SENSITIVE SKIN

Sensitive Skin Magazine is also available online at
www.sensitiveskinmagazine.com.

Publisher/Managing Editor: Bernard Meisler
Editors: Rob Hardin, B. Kold, Steve Horowitz, Ron Kolm & Tim Beckett
Thanks to: Ron Richardson, Patrick O'Neil and Franklin Mount

Front cover: Stephen Lack
Back cover: JD King

You can find us at:
Facebook—**www.facebook.com/sensitiveskin**
Twitter—**www.twitter.com/sensitivemag**
YouTube—**www.youtube.com/sensitiveskintv**

We also publish in various electronic formats (Kindle, PDF, etc.), and have our own lines of books and recordings. For more info about **Sensitive Skin Books**, please go to
www.sensitiveskinmagazine.com/books/
and for **Sensitive Skin Music**, go to
www.sensitiveskinmagazine.com/downloads-store/.

To purchase back issues in printed or PDF format, go to
www.sensitiveskinmagazine.com/back-issues/.

You can contact us at **info@sensitiveskinmagazine.com**.

Submissions: **www.sensitiveskinmagazine.com/submissions**.

This issue is dedicated to the memory of slum goddess Maggie Estep.

ISBN-10: 0983927197
ISBN-13: 978-0-9839271-9-8

Contents

Gladyss of the Hunt

Arthur Nersesian

"Gladyss! Turn on the TV, quick!"

"Hold on!" I muttered, having just been awakened from a sound sleep.

Assuming it had something to do with my murder case, which my brother knew I was assigned to, I put on my glasses and flipped it on.

"What happened?" I asked him groggily, nervous that the killer had struck yet again while I slept. But onscreen I saw Colin Powell, the Secretary of State, speaking in a large auditorium filled with suits.

"What the hell is this?"

"Powell is at the UN, making a case for war so that we'll invade Iraq."

"Carl, I was sleeping!"

"We're being pushed into a war for absolutely no reason. Doesn't that bother you?"

"There's no draft, Carl," I said, turning the TV off. "It's not like Vietnam. No one's going to be forced to fight if they don't want to."

"How about the Iraqi people?" he shouted.

"I gotta go," I said, not caring to debate this bullshit any further.

"Do you mind if I ask you a personal question?"

"I'm still a 23 year old virgin, OK?" I said.

"How's the OCD?"

"All cleared up," I said and hung up. I lay back down. This was why I was glad Carl was no longer living in the city. He'd be breathing down my neck every second, trying to control my life. But I was always worried about him.

I closed my eyes, breathed steadily and tried to push all concerns out of my head. The only thing that stuck in my mind was the vision I'd had in yoga class the other day—a tall, slim, shimmering woman holding a bow and arrow. After a while I showered, dressed, and went off to work. When I arrived, Bernie was sitting at his old partner's desk, resting his head against a cardboard box in front of him.

I peeked to make sure that his shoe was still on, then approached him. "You didn't call One PP about the Marilyn web site, did you?"

"Yep," he said, without making eye contact.

I didn't need the crisp morning light to see that Bernie needed a shave and a change of clothes. He looked haggard. Finally he sat up in his chair, swallowed down whatever bile had risen in his throat and said, "Last night after the credit card theft, I figured that this guy might be targeting me. So I've spent the last eight hours going through all my cases over the last fifteen years." He hit his head against the cardboard box. There were several more boxes on the floor behind the desk.

"Those are all your cases?" I was only a rookie on a thirty-day assignment given to me because I happened to look like his victim, but being a homicide detective was my goal.

"This is decades of pulling rats out of glue traps and putting them into tiny cages upstate. But I came up with nothing."

"So what now?"

"The problem with this business isn't running out of ideas, it's having too many of them. Bert used to say that."

"What ideas?"

He opened the file in front of him. It was our case. Aside from various reports, I saw a stack of crime photos. Close-ups of severed heads. Detailed pictures of wrists and ankles splattered with blood and taped together. Single-digit numbers carved painfully into soft flesh.

"I'm sure you noticed that all the numbers cut into the vic's limbs correspond with the numbers cut into prior vics . . . ." I again made the mistake of stating the obvious.

"Yeah, yeah. The way the bodies are positioned, the numbering on the limbs, the crap he shoves into their hands—all that shit. If you can figure out what it means, I'll give you ten bucks. Otherwise . . ." He made a zipper gesture over his mouth. All these dead ends were evidently driving him nuts.

"The thing I find most interesting is the actual taping," Bernie finally said. "It would be really hard to get their limbs like that and balance them all to stay upright."

"Maybe the guy worked for Mailboxes Etc."

"And why is this the only victim he didn't decapitate?"

"Yet he still did the numbering and taping," I pointed out.

When I looked at the Polaroids of our latest Jane Doe, I gasped. The killer had been so violent that even her implants were sliced apart. Also, unlike the other girls, she had a tattoo on her back—a coiled and sleeping dragon.

"What now?" I asked.

"I'm going to shave, change my shirt and get a coffee. Then we'll go back to the list."

I used the recess to run to the lab, where I gave my baggied cellphone to a techie and asked him to lift Noel's prints from it, then run the prints through the file to see if they matched any we had found at the other crime scenes. He told me the CSI techies had found two new fingerprints at last night's crime scene that they were pretty certain belonged to the killer.

As I got back to the squad room, Alex and Annie arrived, both at the same time. Just when I began to wonder if they were sleeping together, Bernie explained that they had gone out to Brooklyn to check up on some possible leads regarding the latest victim. A wonderful way to spend a Saturday morning, considering they both had families.

"Find out anything?"

> *"Yeah, yeah. The way the bodies are positioned, the numbering on the limbs, the crap he shoves into their hands—all that shit. If you can figure out what it means, I'll give you ten bucks. Otherwise . . ." He made a zipper gesture over his mouth. All these dead ends were evidently driving him nuts.*

"Her real name was Jane Hansen, nickname Minty," Annie said, reading from her notepad. "She lived in Greenpoint with her cat Angus. Went to NYU film school and was still paying off her student loans. She's the first vic who doesn't seem connected to any escort service, though I guess she might be a freelancer."

"But she might not be a hooker at all," Alex added.

"Why do you say that?" Bernie asked.

"She has no record, and we haven't found anything tying her to the sex industry," Annie said, almost happily. I remembered how bad she'd felt when we found so little at the last vic's house.

"Did the receptionist at the Ticonderoga ever see her before?"

"Nope," Annie replied. "And she has no priors of any kind."

"Do me a favor," Bernie said to Alex, handing him a piece of paper with a phone number scribbled on it. "I've called them twice already. This is tech support. Can you stay on them to get us a computer geek? I need someone to look at Gladyss's friend's laptop, check out this, uh, web site, and help determine if our guy is targeting this lady." I wasn't sure why they would need to look at her laptop, but I didn't say anything as Alex took the paper.

With the help of last week's expanded task force, we had whittled down our list of suspects to roughly two dozen names consisting of those we couldn't find or hadn't interviewed yet and three men we had interviewed who were deemed persons of interest, worth interviewing again.

Using details from the Ticonderoga Hotel case, Bernie was now able to cut the list down further, bringing our suspects down to a baker's dozen. They consisted of eight whites, two light-skinned blacks and three Latinos, all of whom could've matched the poor-contrast image of the suspect on the washed-out Ticonderoga tape. All were relatively thin and had a history of theft, frequenting prostitutes and/or violence against women.

"If we can hit these guys," he suggested, "a series of quick field interrogations should give us some idea if any of them is our boy."

I didn't share his optimism about detecting instant guilt. To me it seemed more like a big, chilly fishing expedition. Again I was teamed with Bernie. I didn't know if he took painkillers or simply wore a more comfortable shoe, but he seemed a little less angry this time. As we headed out to his car, I asked him what the plan of attack was.

Again I was teamed with Bernie. I didn't know if he took painkillers or simply wore a more comfortable shoe, but he seemed a little less angry this time.

"You want to know the plan of—" he caught himself. I knew he was about to say something nasty. "OK, unless they're complete psychos—zero affect—these guys are usually right on the edge. Ready to pop. You don't have to press that hard. If they start coming apart, you lock 'em up, sweat 'em, run their prints and check their alibis for the night of the murders."

When I asked him if he could remember his first murder case, he said it involved a drug dealer back when he was "a ghetto cop in the Bushwhack." It sounded like an old *Kojak* rerun.

"The difference is provincialism," he said as we drove up Eighth Avenue. "Out there, you knew your characters and what they were up to. Manhattan is different. Everyone's just blowing through," he said just as an arctic gust blasted down the avenue, tagging any flesh left exposed by poorly wrapped scarves and the bright pink earlobes of those who didn't pull their hats down tight enough.

"Was Youngblood just blowing through?" I inquired, remembering the geriatric tube sock hustler. Since Bernie seemed in a relatively good mood, I thought maybe he would open up a bit. But he didn't hear me.

"I was just too young to know any better," he muttered.

"What should you have known?"

"A cute young teenager gets into drugs. The boyfriend who got her hooked leaves her. Her dealer moves up to being her pimp. To avoid going away for her third conviction, she becomes your own private ghost. I was a lonely kid—not much older than you—who made the mistake of getting too close to a beautiful, damaged girl. Same as Bert, only at his age he should've known a lot better."

"Bert, your old partner?"

"Yeah, except he married his snitch. Mine was found in the bottom of a filthy air shaft out in the Red Hook." He paused a moment, and I could see by the way he chewed his inner lip that he was reliving the moment. "I've had to spend the last twenty years knowing it was my stupidity that put her down there."

Bernie's cell rang; it was Alex to say that tech support at One Police Plaza was a little backed up, but someone would definitely look into the web site by tomorrow.

Of the six remaining suspects Bernie and I were checking, we knew we'd be lucky if we got to the three most promising ones today. All had been in prison within the past five years. Two of them, Joseph

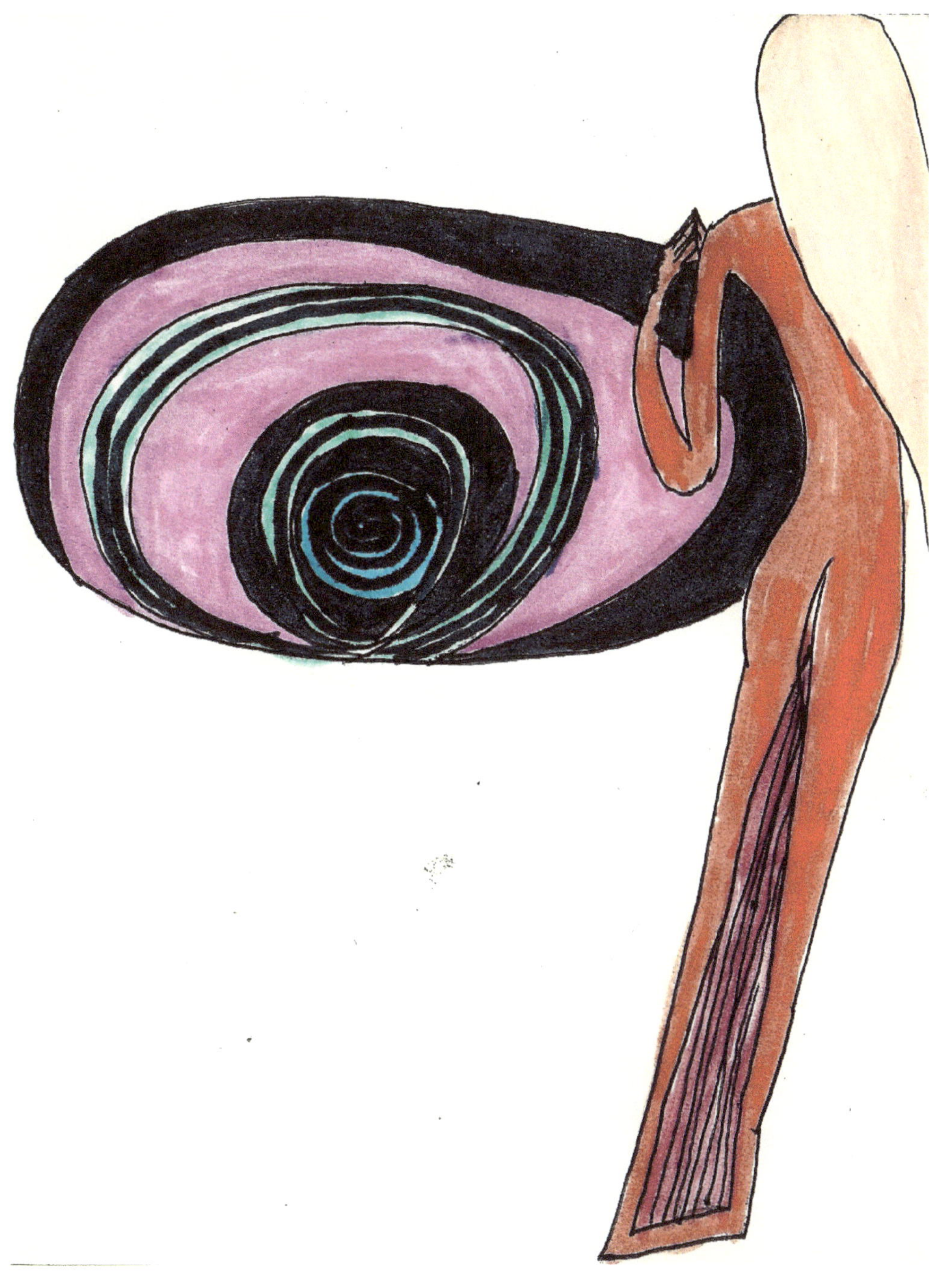

Vo-tex, painting by David West

have a particularly vengeful place in his heart for pimps who killed their hookers.

What's more, Sprag had also been arrested a few years before on a murder charge involving ligature strangulation—a girl named Sally DiNasio was found with a telephone cord wrapped around her neck. She was a Garden State runaway whom he'd probably recruited at Port Authority. Although the case went to trial, he got off due to insufficient evidence. He was later arrested for drug possession and did the majority of his twelve-year sentence, though he shortened it somewhat by informing on another inmate.

According to his parole officer, Sprag worked for a few months at the Forty Second Street Partnership, a halfway house for early releases. He was one of those guys who wears a white jumpsuit and sweeps the streets around Times Square. Then one day he stopped showing up for work and coming to meetings. The parole officer explained, "I have a warrant out on his ass, but haven't had time to hunt him down."

Sprag's last known address was a transient hotel,

Donnelly and Nessun O'Flaherty, had done time for assaulting hookers, but the last and best suspect was a pimp named Howard Sprag who went by the moniker "Hozec." Bernie explained that this nickname was a shortening of either Whore Executive or Whore Executioner—Sprag was rumored to wring the necks of his bottom earners. Bernie seemed to the Lathem, at Twenty-Eighth and Tenth. As we parked in front of the place, Bernie said he had interviewed another suspect here just last week during the initial dragnet. The desk clerk, a tall Indian gentleman named Lionel, recognized Bernie as he entered.

"How can I be of service, Detective?"

When Bernie asked him if Howard Sprag still lived there, Lionel paused, sighed and responded in a watered-down British accent, "About two months ago, Mr. Sprag called down to the desk saying there was a dead body in his room. I went upstairs and saw him standing in the hall smoking a cigarette. When I asked about said body, he just nodded toward his room. I went in, looked around, peeked under the bed and told him I didn't see any dead body. 'It's out the window,' he replied. I figured he was pulling my leg, you know. So I went back downstairs. By the time I reached the lobby, someone out front was screaming. Apparently Mr. Sprag finished his fag and jumped out of the window."

Mr. Sprag called down to the desk saying there was a dead body in his room. I went upstairs and saw him standing in the hall smoking a cigarette. When I asked about said body, he just nodded inside his room. I went in, looked around, peeked under the bed, and told him I didn't see any dead body. 'It's out the window,' he replied. I figured he was pulling my leg, you know. So I went back downstairs. By the time I reached the lobby someone out front was screaming. Apparently Mr. Sprag finished his fag and jumped out of the window."

"Rest in peace, Hozec," I muttered.

"Why doesn't his PO know this shit?" Bernie asked no one in particular.

"You're the first person who's come around asking about him," Lionel replied. Bernie asked when this had happened exactly, and Lionel's answer told us Sprag had been dead before the last two murders were committed.

Joe Donnelly was next up. For a brief time, he had been a member of the infamous Irish gang, the Westies, but they reportedly tossed him out when it became clear he had a greater loyalty to heroin. More recently Donnelly had been living in and out of his mother's place in the Penn South Housing Projects, Section Eight Assistance, along Twenty-Fourth and Eighth Avenue. Bernie recalled arresting him for something once before. Maybe extortion.

"So maybe he has it in for you," I pointed out, referring to his stolen credit card.

"Maybe," he replied.

We parked in front of the building, got in the front door without ringing, went up the stairs, and knocked on his mother's door. Bernie was a big believer in the surprise drop-in.

"In here, pronto," a deep, hoarse voice hollered. The place was a mess, and smelled of sardines and boiled eggs. A bloated Raggedy Anne from hell seemed to be parked permanently inches in front of a loud and angry TV set, a half-empty 40 of Coors and a box of saltines on a table beside her chair.

"You're not Meals on Wheels," she growled.

"And you're not Vanessa Del Rio doing Desire Cousteau," he replied. I had no idea who he was talking about.

“The TV is *not* loud, so don’t tell me it is!” she said defiantly when we identified ourselves.

“We’re not here for that,” Bernie shot back and turned it off. “We’re looking for that evil shit that you let loose upon the world.”

“Ain’t here.”

Bernie pulled out his pistol and kicked open her closet and bathroom doors, checking for himself.

“Joey’s a good kid,” she replied. “What’s he done now?”

“Killed some girls.”

“Huh?”

“Dead girls,” I repeated to her.

“When’s he s’posed to have killed ’em?” she asked.

“Where the fuck is he?” Bernie shouted.

“My kidneys are killing me,” she complained. “I need dialysis.”

“Where the fuck is your kid?”

“That’s what I’m trying to tell youse. He’s been in Riker’s for six months now—shoplifting.”

Bernie used his cell to call the prison and confirm it. Two down.

“Now can I watch the rest of my shows?” she asked, turning the TV back on.

“It’s too loud,” I said, turning it down.

“I can’t hear it like that.”

“Get a hearing aid,” I shouted.

As soon as we stepped into the hallway, the volume shot back up. At least I’d given her a little exercise—she’d had to lift the remote again.

When we returned to the car, Bernie looked at the info sheet for suspect number three and saw that he was still on parole.

“Christ, it’s dark,” I said, amazed that it was already pitch black even though it was only late afternoon. I was fired up about interrogating the other suspects but by now, Bernie’s foot was clearly agitating the hell out of him.

“Let’s call it a night and try to reach his parole officer tomorrow,” I suggested. That would be the state parole office on Fortieth Street. “All right,” he said.

We returned to the precinct where Bernie suddenly realized he was way behind on the paperwork needed for a court case tomorrow morning. He took a Valium to handle the pain, but as soon as he sat down, he passed out with his head on his desk.

My phone rang: it was the lab tech with the test results I’d asked for. Noel’s prints didn’t match anyone of the ones found at the various crime scenes. So much for my theory.

It wasn’t the end of my shift yet, so I grabbed Bernie’s paperwork and spent the next hour and a half trying to extract vital information from him so I could finish his paperwork. Otherwise a homicide charge would get dropped the next day.

* * *

“Is this the squad that investigates Hollywood stud muffins?”

O’Ryan popped his head round the door. He told me he’d just finished logging in a box of stolen iPods in the property room downstairs. Even though Bernie was snoring away on the couch. I walked out into the hall to talk with Eddie.

“My cell phone died, I’m really sorry,” he said referring to my date night with Noel. Then he asked if the actor’s fingerprints had matched anything.

“No,” I replied. “But you still could’ve called me the next morning to see how I was doing.”

“I heard that you roughed up some boy reporter at the Ticonderoga Hotel, so I figured you were doing fine,” he replied.

Before he could get around to asking if I wanted to go to dinner, his temporary partner, Lenny, suddenly appeared and the two had to run. I finished Bernie’s paperwork and headed to yoga, leaving Bernie sleeping in the office.

an excerpt from **Gladyss of the Hunt**

Silent Calls

Sparrow

Silent Calls

You know how sometimes the phone rings and when you answer it no one's there? Many of those calls are made by cats.

Marriage Mistake

"My big mistake was that I married two men, but not at the same time!" Gail remarked.

Science Virgin

"I'm a science virgin," said Adele. "I've never conducted an experiment!"

Exercise "Surgery"

Before plastic surgery, movie actors would perform facial exercises to improve their appearance. Humphrey Bogart spent four years with the Anderssen Method of mouth exercise, in his early 20s.

Singing Furniture

My furniture is singing a tune from Scriabin.

Extreme

"I work in the growing field of Extreme Retail," Dory revealed.

Not Watching

I don't have a TV set, but often I'll get the television listings from *The New York Times,* just to find out what I'm not watching at any given moment. For example, right now I'm missing *Extra Cheese,* a reality show about pizza-making.

Sleepshopping

"Not only am I a sleepwalker, but I'm also a sleepshopper," Susan revealed. "Last night, while sound asleep, I bought a box of toothpicks and a lightbulb."

Retire into Virtue

"Many rogues and criminals retire into virtue," Patrice observed. "When you get to a certain age, virtue is the only option."

$72

"My father gave me $72 with the stipulation that I spend it in 72 places," Johnny explained. "It took me nine months, but I did it!"

Last Judgment

Why does "The Last Judgment" include the adjective "last"? Was there a First Judgment? Or a Third? Shouldn't it just be called "The Judgment"?

photograph by Chris Bava

New Paintings

Stephen Lack

Expressionist, impressionist, symbolist. Pop imbued with guilt, political outrage, occasional indignation, existential disconnection and an overriding sense of loss. These works celebrate where I have been with tenderness, saying goodbye to a fragile but rich reality.

—*Stephen Lack*

ADMITS KILL

Caravaggio, Baby

Deborah Pintonelli

I have a date with Henry Henderson. We worked together one long summer canvassing for Greenpeace. Yes, I was one of those annoying young people who stop you on the street when you are rushing to your next appointment. He was hot then, now not so much, looking rather fat but with a very good job in city government. After looking at his Facebook photo, I had friended him begrudgingly, but only because we were old mates. I did not tell him I was pregnant. We had gone through, at the end of summer, the quickie abortion experience at a non-profit clinic. One of more than a few I have had, all fathered by partners in super-intense love affairs.

Henry. The first guy who ever went down on me as I held his fistful of curls. The moment he got his pants off it was as if he had never done it before. The excitement would make him go all pale and sweaty, and I would secretely worry he may have a fainting spell or worse. Quick to orgasm, full of chat during sex and,afterwards, he just couldn't get enough of me. Or about five other girls we worked with during that time. It was all in good fun. He was the rare boy who was a real gent and lover of women. There was nothing a woman could do to put him off—menstruation, moods, peeing, bloating, nervousness, difficulty in bed—nothing. He held my hand tight while we waited our turn for the procedure, and bought me ice cream afterwards. Paid for it, bought me dinner, invited me to his parent's place in Sag Harbor.

Henry. The first guy who ever went down on me as I held his fistful of curls. The excitement would make him go all pale and sweaty, and I would secretely worry he may have a fainting spell or worse.

Thinking about him also made me think about the others, the men I let get away. There was always a reason, or so I thought, but the real issue was always that I wasn't, and don't think I ever have been, in love. If that seems sad, well, it sort of is. It doesn't make any sense to have had so many chances and still not have it. Henry, as far as I can tell, didn't have it either. So, while I considered myself to be supremely more attractive, I also thought of us as a pair. Of losers. I knew he was only agreeing to give me advice because he wanted to see me, the "absolutely stunning" girl he used to bang.

I ask him to meet me at Maryann's on the Bowery, where I feel we will have some privacy. Is a newly pregnant woman allowed to wear leather leggings? Why, yes, she is. And a sweet cream colored silk blouse, hair tousled, lips the new/old shade of red everyone is wearing again. A scarf, pashmina, one of five bought in Tokyo. The baby blue one. And heels. Eat your heart out, Henry Henderson. The air is still brisk, and summer seems as if it will never arrive as I walk from my apartment to the restaurant. God, how I love my neighborhood! Where Maryann's is, not so much, though the bit right by the Public Theater is magical. Walking on Broadway past where the Tower Records used to be. When people still shopped for things like CDs and movies. I still see it there. The old places don't fade from memory, they are carried in the heart and mind forever. The moon is just peeping out of a sapphire sky as I hobble over the cobblestones past the fire station on Third. How long will I be able to wear heels? My hair is truly luxuriant, what people say happens to hair with hormones flowing. I am nervous now. Am I supposed to even enterain the idea of fucking him, just to be polite? I have never done it with a fat man.

After we are seated at our table I realize I may have underestimated him. He looks pretty important. And smarter than I remember, which is good because I need his help, but bad because I have to work harder to hide my true feelings, as if I have joined Daddy Warbucks for dinner. Does this make me Annie? Should I later sit on his knee and ask for a present? I think too that I should leave my options open about sleeping with him. Who cares about his size? I remember all of the good things about him now as he peers at me through his glasses.

"Liz? Are you alright?"

"Yes! But it's been so long since I . . . ."

Time for the daily glass of red.

"I know! I've been keeping an eye on you, though."

"You have! Well, I don't do much of interest, just work."

"You haven't changed. Looking better, if I may say so."

"You may. Thank you."

I don't comment on how he has changed and he notices, says, "I'm different. Hope it isn't too much of a shock." There is an iced bowl of raw carrots, celery, and olives on the table and I take one of each, nibble, shrug, change the subject. His face softens, he sees I don't care, and we move on to other subjects. I lean back on the red leather banquette to better survey the room, make sure there are not any familiar faces. No one I know is there. No one I know comes to these places anymore, the haunts of our not-so-distant youth. Indochine. Esther's. Now people were more inclined to go elsewhere.

My cravings thus far take me to only one place: meat and potato land. There is a porterhouse on the menu so I order it, with potatoes Anna. Henry has the blackened salmon caesar. It is a fine night and I am suprised how much I am enjoying his company, the place, the safeness of dwelling a bit in the past. So much lately has been new and jarring. He tells me that what we need to go over has to be done in private. He lives nearby, on Tenth Street. He suggests taking a cab to his place and I am glad, the leather and heels will not do for another walk. He pays for dinner, which was delicious. I am done gnawing on the bone and have sucked every last droplet of juice out of it and need no dessert.

On the way there, I check my messages and see there are texts from all of the usual suspects. Henry is checking on his stuff as well, and I see his jaw in profile and remember the man I used to know. Kind, determined, a bit on edge always. He smokes now, and there is a pack in his hand at the ready for when we exit the taxi. As we arrive I notice he does not live on my favorite block, but a little further east, near St. Mark's Church. He has the first floor of a narrow brownstone, with a working fireplace and shiny wood floors. Bookcases floor to ceiling line the wall opposite the fireplace. The small kitchen, done in fancy stainless and granite, is spotless and looks rarely used.

"You like?"

"I do! It's a real adult's home."

"Yeah, remember the dump I lived in near school?"

His apartment at 114th and Broadway was above a Chinese-Cuban restaurant and always smelled of garlic. I recall he owned one futon, a dresser, a broken-down sofa and a television set. I ask him for a cup of tea before he offers me a drink. Then we are sitting very close together on his leather sofa, and he has his hand on my leg. I don't ask him about his current love life, or even if he has been married and divorced, or anything else. I am just keen on this feeling of comfort with this most unlikely of persons.

I don't think I've had sex sober since I was a teenager, and I can't even remember what it's like. He gets up to fix himself another drink and I see he is not quite as large as I thought. Or, he seems less so because I have been forming this other opinion of him, based on less concrete criteria. His kindness, the clear, concise gaze he fixes upon me, the way I seem to be someone else to him, i.e., my other, earlier self, all of this gets thrown into the mix. When we go to bed, it seems perfectly natural and I stay the night, sleeping peacefully in his sparsely furnished bedroom darkened by earthy velvet curtains, my hand resting curled on his lump of a stomach. We have entered an unexpected zone, but I am not nervous about it. I don't know if it's him, or the hormones, or both. He sleeps well, too, and I sense he is not surprised by any of it. It has taken me this long to figure out he has sensed my desperation and responded to it like some lover of stray cats. Is that what men like him do, await their opportunity? And why not? I know I do.

I don't think I've had sex sober since I was a teenager, and I can't even remember what it's like.

The next morning I am off with a smile and a kiss, a queasy, not-right feeling in my stomach. Like cramps, as in before my period comes. I haven't been to the doctor yet, taking it upon myself to procrastinate, as I am healthy and in no rush to be tied to regular visits and dietary restrictions. But now this seems urgent. I see spots of blood in the toilet, and I feel worse by the minute. I call in sick, something I never do, and then call my doctor. No appointments, they say, but I force them to make one, claiming an emergency, the urgency in my voice getting through to the plump receptionist with too-long hair who wears no make-up. "Rosa, I need to see her today. I'll wait there as long as it takes." I'm throwing on jeans, a sweater, flat shoes. I call my friend Tina and tell her what's up. "Oh, no! Sweetie, it's probably nothing." Well, I say, it doesn't feel like nothing, it feels like something. "Don't let anyone bother me, OK?" I'm not good in a crisis, I start cleaning things in a hyper-OCD manner when I'm supposed to be leaving: I decide the bathroom rug is dirty and a spray of bleach on all of the kitchen counters is imperative. As I leave I see I have bleach stains on my jeans and sweater, but it's too late to change.

Dr. Judy Nathan is near the flatiron building, a short cab ride away. I've put a pad in place and feel it getting moist and warm. I am not nice to the cab driver, who decides to take a leisurely ride past Union Square instead of going up Fifth Avenue. I will not tip him, am tempted to get out without paying as we pull up to the building office. Now the summer we have been waiting for has finally come and the sweater I am wearing, bleachy and sticking to my skin, feels absolutely disgusting. My hair is stuck to my forehead and I am in danger of crying in public, another thing I have almost never done. This from the girl with balls—what they say you have to have to do or be anything great—who rarely leaves home without them.

Dr. Nathan is from Pakistan, married to a Jew who is ten years older than me and looks much younger. She tells me I am not pregnant. At least not at this particular moment.

"Why didn't you come to see me sooner?" She asks.

"Well, I took the test, and . . . ." I really had no good reason.

"This is going to require an outpatient D and C. Do you have the time today?"

Sure, nothing but time is what I have.

She is giving me her stern look, but also smiling as she snaps off her rubber gloves.

"It's nothing to worry about, just a precautionary measure."

I am still prone on the examining table, legs apart. She tells me I can sit up and get dressed, she will return momentarily. The room I am in is the typical small, poorly lit box one would expect. As I put my clothes on I feel the tears coming again, this time out of embarrassment and shame. She is going to tell me I am not ever going to be pregnant, my time has passed, and like so many women who thought they could wait, I waited too long. She finds me in this state when she returns, and as always, I am glad she is my doctor.

"These things happen, my dear. The fetus was just not viable. The body rejects the embryo, and this is a good thing, for who knows what was wrong?"

I imagine something dead inside me, malformed, pitiful. I want it out. I had just been thinking about times when I didn't want to be pregnant. Now here I was wanting to be but I wasn't. I don't know if I can handle the nuances at this point.

"Is there any way of knowing?"

"No. Not in these cases. You have to be at least in your second trimester to do the tests. Which, if you are planning to try this again, you should have, at your age."

I say nothing, and she decides it's time to give me a hug and asks, "Are you OK on all of your meds?"

She means the Ambien and the Xanax. The Lipitor. "Yes."

"If you are really serious about this, you know you need to consult me on what to take, you can't just go on popping the pills."

It's funny, the ways she says 'popping the pills,' her lovely accent making the Ps sound like Bs. I start to laugh and fear it will turn into hysterical cackling at any moment. Along with tears. She pats me on the back like the poor old pup that I am. "You'll be OK. Just come to me sooner next time, OK?"

"OK."

I don't know who to call. I am feeling small and helpless and wanting my bedroom, or a darker, tighter space to be in. Which is exactly what I get at New York-Presbyterian: a hot and stuffy room outfitted with all of the machinery needed to inspect my uterus and remove the foreign object. The lighting is crypto-disco, dark with flashing silver power source buttons and green LED numbers on black backgrounds. The technicians seem like aliens in white coats adjusting spacecraft knobs and levers, not very concerned about whether what they are working on is human or machine. I've been this route before, know the drill, don't take offense at the inhumanity of it all and, most importantly, know I will be famished afterwards. The doctor in charge is a bland young man who barely speaks to me and calls me "Ma'am." Irreverently I plot my impending visit to Katz's Deli. Tender slices of rosy-colored bliss await. He tells me I will be allowed to rest for an hour there, and then I will be free to go. But I probably shouldn't eat. IDGAF, I'm eating!

I endure the sounds of the vacuuming of my innards with as much grace as possible. There is a disturbing pressure that lifts your middle up, then shakes it around a bit, as a dog might do with a toy. You feel like you need to pee, or worse. A nurse, the only one who seems remotely human, helps the doctor. She has tired eyes and is wearing a smock bearing colorful teddy bears. Patting my arm, she says, "almost finished," and I want to hug her. It's not supposed to hurt, but it does. Is it imagined pain? The machine beeps and we are through, the suctiony, washing-machine sounds it emits ending. I think of procedures like this being done around the country, often in places where the doctors and patients are threatened by wackos. I remember reading in Susan Brownmiller's *In Our Time* about pre-legal times when women started their own clinics, did this procedure from their homes with crude apparati like lengths of rubber tubing and catheters.

I am reminded of one of my favorite paintings by Caravaggio, a still life of a sleeping infant floating on a pure black background, as if the figure was a ship sailing on a dark, angry sea. I found it on a trip to Florence while away for a semester abroad. I was pregnant then, too, and about to have my first abortion in Rome, of all places. The painting is startlingly modern because of the wonderful contrasts of light and dark; so impious, so different from the other paintings in the room. The pearly white of its body is streaked with pink and other iridescent hues, like a sea creature. The baby appears bloated, a bit grotesque, and from the guidebook you learn that Caravaggio used a dead infant as a model.

I remember thinking about it as I sobbed on the grass near some parked cars outside of the clinic in Rome after that abortion. The full moon was in a sky the color of a cheap sharkskin suit. I went to a trattoria afterwards with the remaining two girls who would still speak to me after everyone had found out what I was going to do. We ate arrancini and drank a whole bottle of wine. We were gorgeous and free and so young. Later we danced to the Rolling Stones in a basement bar because that's what the Italians liked, the Stones and jazz. We met some guys, one of whom remarked how pale I was. I couldn't, nor did I think I ever wanted to again, have sex. You were a visitor there. You did the things people wanted you to do. Most of the time.

an excerpt from To the Last Gay Man I Will Ever Love

Ballad of a Lousy Husband

Joshua Mohr

I should probably tell you more about the night Blue pushed me off the bar because that was really when our marriage ended. Sure, we stayed together another nine, twelve, maybe fifteen months more, but nothing was ever good again. She stopped thinking it was possible to make me a man, thought that I was a lost cause, and she was right.

I was super-coked up and had at least ten Fernets swimming in me already when I met Blue and a couple of her girlfriends. I'd been bartending around the corner and got off at midnight and walked in Laszlo and knew the guys slinging drinks pretty well, Rick and Brian, who had a whole *Brokeback Mountain* thing going on, except instead of illicit fishing trips they blew dunes of coke and probably slow danced while the sun came up, much to the chagrin of Brian's wife.

I walk in and kiss Blue and say hey to her friends and immediately went to the bar to buy a round, had a quick pop of Fernet with the Brokeback brigade and struck up a conversation with the woman next to me, some debutante all dressed up and slumming it in the Mission. I dealt with these posh ladies all the time on the weekends, turning our neighborhood into the Dirty Marina—the rich seeing how the paupers lived—and I sort of hated them but also sort of dug making them want to screw me and cocaine made me a kind of charming chauvinist who some women found irresistible and apparently this lady was one of them, because she flirted right off, and I looked her up and down and she wore these crazy jeweled shoes that looked like chandeliers and I—as if deciding to chase a liquored-up impulse to torch those Christmas trees—now needed to drink whiskey from one of her chandelier shoes ASAP.

Which I said to her, making her giggle and bite her bottom lip, and I said, "What's funny?" and she said, "You're crazy," and I said, "You've got that right, pretty lady," and leaned down, slipping off one of her shoes with my wife in a corner having no idea that I was being such a scumbag, simply chatting with her friends, waiting for me to come back with a round of drinks, enjoying a normal night cocktailing until the moment she couldn't stand me anymore, though that was still minutes away, me trying to convince one of the Brokeback blokes to pour whiskey straight into this girl's shoe and either Rick or Brian asking her, "You OK with this?" She pointed at me and said, "He's thirsty," and Rick/Brian poured whiskey in her chandelier, my chalice, and the music thumped some Chicago break beats, and most people at the bar started cheering when I brought the shoe to my lips and slurped

I dealt with these posh ladies all the time on the weekends, turning our neighborhood into the Dirty Marina—the rich seeing how the paupers lived—and I sort of hated them but also sort of dug making them want to screw me and cocaine made me a kind of charming chauvinist who some women found irresistible . . .

painting by Peter Shear

out all the booze and the woman whose shoe it was clapped and made some sorority-style squeals and I held the chandelier up in victory and asked the debutante if she wanted to dance and she said, "Sure," and I said, "Not here," and she said, "Where?"

I still had her chandelier in my hand and I knocked on the bar with it and said, "Up there," and she squealed again and I jumped up on the bar and pulled her up there too and we let the music take over, dancing terribly, me using the chandelier as a prop, flying it all about, doing my whole king-of-the-bar shtick, dancing with spirits and blow and a squealing debutante.

I never saw her coming. One second I was dancing and zooming the shoe in zigzags and the next feeling pressure on the backs of my legs. Feet leaving the bar. Weight flipping in a slow-motion tumble that seemed impervious to gravity.

I wonder if Blue saw me herself or if one of her friends had to point toward the bar and ask, "Is that your husband up there?"

I wonder what went through her mind turning to look, having witnessed countless of my idiotic shenanigans already, each of them tangling together to create a huge disappointing ball, an avalanche of humiliations, too much for one innocent wife to take until it was over, I was over, we were over, I'd gone too far, not with the outlandishness of this one incident, per se, drinking from a chandelier shoe and dancing on a bar, but now the ball was a speeding boulder of all the times I embarrassed Blue, and I bet she didn't even answer her friend, bet she simply stood and stormed as all the ire coursed through her and out her fingertips.

I never saw her coming. One second I was dancing and zooming the shoe in zigzags and the next feeling pressure on the backs of my legs.

Feet leaving the bar.

Weight flipping in a slow-motion tumble that seemed impervious to gravity.

I must have dropped the chandelier, must have brought my hands up to protect my face, must have thought it was the debutante's beau or a jilted one-night stand, it never even occurred to me that Blue might have masterminded this violent fate: still falling, still feeling my legs whipping up until I was upside down.

Crashing face-first to the floor.

And then it was like the whole room vanished.

All the other people gone.

Music nixed.

Just me and the shoe-chandelier sitting on the floor in the empty bar. Blue standing above us. The look in her eyes was all anger. At me. At this drunk she'd tethered herself to. At this person too dense to treat other people with dignity.

I lay there bleeding some with my head all sideways, shocked but also sort of proud of all our life's anarchy. Loved the shoves I never saw coming.

I was rabid with selfishness and the only thing to do with an animal like that was to Old Yeller his ass, point the gun at his head through your tears, pull that trigger and bury the body before he had the chance to hurt you again, leave the tiny chandelier as a headstone, a beacon, a lighthouse, tossing watts to mark the grave of a lousy husband.

A whimpering eulogy flitting on the wind, in memory of a parasite, a wrecking ball, a waste.

1971

Celia Farber

Anyway I had a goldfish, a common Woolworth's goldfish, which I brought home in a water filled plastic bag, and somebody, a man named Rick, I think, who worked for my father, said it would be safe to place him in a concrete planter on the terrace, filled with water. Everybody is always doing their best. I remember his kind and comforting energy and I think he had been a marine.

I named my goldfish Simon. I loved him, but I can't swear he had any real feelings for me. I turned him into my best friend, confided in him. It was the year my life collapsed. I was six, and my mother had disappeared.

I named my goldfish Simon. I loved him, but I can't swear he had any real feelings for me. I turned him into my best friend, confided in him. It was the year my life collapsed. I was six, and my mother had disappeared.

Every morning, having bolted down the spiral staircase carrying my mother's portrait, asking anybody I could find if she had *called,* being rebuffed, I would go sit on the edge of that planter and stroke Simon's tail through the water.

One morning I came out and found him curled up in the drain hole, the water gone. I can still see his small orange body curled up in there, defeated.

I don't think I cried then. But strangely enough I cried today, in a cold cafe in Bushwick, Brooklyn, with waterfalls on the walls, and people working on their laptops. I was already coming apart, from the night before, but now I started to experience what felt like *Simon's* emotions from 1971. Could that be?

Pain seared right through my heart that felt dark blue and like a thread, weaving a telegram from childhood that was never delivered at the time. I gripped my own throat, pushed up against my jawbone and tried to block the tears. Simon would not have understood *why* the water was leaving. He would have been wondering why I had let this happen to him and didn't protect him. He would feel betrayed, so deeply betrayed, just as I had. And he had no chance.

I always wondered exactly what time it happened.

Survey 30, acrylic gouache on paper, Tom McGlynn

The Earring

Alan Kaufman

I FIRST SAW THE GOLD CRESCENT OF RENEGADE freedom dangling from the lobe of a nameless hairy hippy Goy, his scrawny, insolent neck bound by a red bandanna. He leaned with outthrust hip of impertinent American coolness against the miniature white plaster-like Arc D'Triumph that looms in meager solemnity over the leafy green, daggered streetlamps of Washington Square Park. Over his back he'd slung a guitar, hung by a strap embroidered with flower patterns. He smoked a cigarette and with his long-fingered, filthy hand tossed aside the long, limp, unwashed strands of hair from his face to better show off the earring. I just stood there agape.

Not that I hadn't seen earrings on men. It was just that now my eyes were wide open, I was ready to be pierced. The coming prospect of my high school graduation inspired me to piracy. I was a Sinbad waiting to bust loose, a Crimson Pirate aching for a ship. At night, I sat at the edge of my bed with scissors, razors, shoe polish, ammonia, rags, hacking at the cuffs and collars and sleeves of all my clothes, defacing, shredding them, purposefully soiling and smudging and ripping and bleaching out their loser quality of 'good boy' conformity, teasing forth their buried gypsy essence of repressed daring-do, brutalizing them into fadedness. I tried to make them look as though they'd been worn for years of endless rebellious sun-beaten road travel, each loosed thread unleashing the dormant cowboy in my Bronx-crushed soul. For I was dying to leave the brick madhouse of ancestral guilt and mass murder memories in which I had grown up, strike out on my own across the western highways of America, reach some land of uncoralled freedom where no one had ever heard of Auschwitz or lay in fart-enshrouded, Yiddish-whispering defeat, agonizing over unpaid bills and gallstones.

It was only a matter of time before I could leave. Turning eighteen and a high school diploma would make the sundering of my mother's apron strings official. I was college-bound with Simon and Garfunkel in my soul. I couldn't wait to hit the City College campus running. So that, in the pocket of whatever shirt I happened to wear, I kept folded the now quite tattered acceptance letter from City College of New York: my passport out. For to me Manhattan might as well have been California, the Beach Boy's surfing songs lullabies of Broadway. Whatever wasn't the Bronx was Annette Funicello country, a golden land of singing promise, opportunity's Nirvana was but a subway ride downtown away. With the admissions letter, I was eligible to apply for student loans which would, in effect, liberate me from the necessity to work. With it I could earn my degree under the new Open Admissions policy for only fifty-eight dollars per semester. At City College I could smoke pot, drink wine, wear my hair long, fuck coeds, write novels and discover the meaning of life.

Now I was rarely home anymore. It wasn't really home now anyway, more a hostel for neanderthalic wayfarers. I looked upon my parents and brother as the primitive inhabitants of some Stone Age household among whom I had happened to plop down in my embryonic time machine. We barely grunted to each other. They moved like shadows, with jutting, shelf-like brows, flesh-and-blood Flintstones, preoccupied with their meat-gathering and laundry.

I left for school two hours early each day and arrived uptown at Dewitt Clinton High School at 7AM, an hour when only the janitor and one or two fanatically devoted teachers were to be found about the premises. I trudged upstairs to the tiny bell tower office of the *Magpie*, the school literary magazine, on which I now served as editor-in-chief, and sat plucking at my earlobe, wondering if I dared take the last, final step that for once and all would expel me from the claw-like grip of my parents, the Bronx, the Holocaust,

Jewishness—even my own idea of myself.

For I wanted to feel brand new, not two thousand years old, and the earring seemed to be the way. to do that. Just the thought of it opened my ear, exponentially expanded my spiritual acoustics, made me hear as if for the first time the thrumming growing sound that had been hemorrhaging around me from airwaves and stereos and lips and street corner-thumped guitars, of Dylan and the Doors, the Rolling Stones, Neil Young—a harmonica and bottleneck steel string sound of rocking blues America, revolutionizing catgut folk locomotive songs, drugs sex and fuck you Mister Jones, the sound of politically ignorant, passion-thrilling clenched-fist rebellion and righteousness in the hearts of teen kids rioting across the land.

Somehow, I had not heard this sound before, though it had been all around me, this swelling tumult blasting down the barrier wall of my darkling mind, a mind that was after years of parental and public school incarceration a prison yard still bounded by the silk of the Motown Sound, the Temptations and Smoky Robinson, Marvin Gaye and Ray Charles. Elvis, well, he was too white bread-yokel sounding for this Bronx kid, and I just couldn't relate to the Beatles. When I bopped down the Grand Concourse in my Clinton Football Jersey over sharp slacks and pointed black cockroach-killer shoes, it was Isaac Hayes that played in my head, not the Beatles.

But on that night, out in the Village, while walking around without knowing a single living soul or with any understanding of why I was there, I saw the earring and it opened my ear and I grew desperate. I needed to do something now, before graduation, something nutty and outrageous that would declare my independence. I wanted my parents to know and see, in a way that nothing else would demonstrate, how completely free of them I was about to become.

I was growing my hair long, yes, strands at a time, a commando raid of follicular revolt. At each subsequent haircut, I asked the barber to leave it a bit longer, then coming home to see what my parents would say. Just now, it was over my ears, but just barely, and this hadn't really earned more then a disgusted grunt from my cigar-dazed father and, from my mother, no comment at all. Lately, I had bought a peacoat too, to affect a more Bohemian look; even now, I wore Frye boots, though my football coaches had warned against their bad affect on the foot.

Not that I hadn't seen earrings on men. It was just that now my eyes were wide open, I was ready to be pierced. The coming prospect of my high school graduation inspired me to piracy.

To get the earring, I called Arnold Razumny, my old schoolmate, who now ran, ear-pierced, with a pack of ear-pierced junkies, snorting heroin and nodding out in each other's living rooms.

"Whassup, Big Man?" he asked with an affected jive accent.

"I'm cool, I'm cool. Hey, man, check this out: Where'd you get your ear pierced?"

There was a pause. Followed by: "You joining the earring elite, my man?"

"Thinking about it."

"Well, stop thinking and check out Bobby-Ann's earring store on Fordham Road. She'll make you a hole, no problem. It's not a biggie, my man, not a biggie, they do it just about every day. Go in there, slap down your fifteen bucks. You go in a cherry, and go out a gold-studded dude!"

photograph by Ted Barron

Bobby-Ann's was not what I imagined, though. No Aquarian psychedelic enclave this: sandwiched between the conservative shoe stores and Army Navy emporiums that lined Fordham Road, it was a real store for real women's earrings. All the girls behind the counter were dressed in the sort of lime-green smocks worn by dental assistants. The place was a strange blend of jewelry store and surgical theater.

When I entered the place it went dead silent. All the women looked up. A girl my age with a kittenish face asked, "Can I help you?"

Red-faced I said: "What-do-I gotta-do ta-get my-ear . . . ya-know...pierced?"

The other women were still watching, one or two now with greater interest.

"SAN-DYYY!" the counter girl shouted. From behind the screened-off rear of the shop, a place ablaze with stainless steel lights, came rushing a chunky Irish freckled woman with green eyes penciled black like Elizabeth Taylor in *Cleopatra,* her enormous breasts wobbling in a doctor's smock. She asked the nodding counter girl "Is this the one?", took my hand in hers and dragged me into the back past a row of chagrined and envious faces, saying: "Right this way, honey. You want your ear pierced? Sandy's gonna do you like you never been done before!"

"My friend Arnie sent me," I said lamely.

"Never heard of him." She shoved me down into a chair. "Stay put," she said.

She whipped out a black velvet-lined tray imbedded with various gold and silver earrings and posts. "So, whatddaya like? You look like a post guy to me. Posts are cute for short-haired fellahs."

Heart racing, I said: "I wanna crescent."

"But you don't have long hair!"

That news crushed me. Somehow I'd imagined that the carefully cultivated slightly longish curls and waves gathering blackly around my face was a free-flying flag. Now I knew for certain: no one was fooled. I was as square as a Rubik's cube.

"Well, gimme a crescent anyway," I said, defiantly. "Because I'm growing my hair long. It's already started, you just can't see because I made the decision just a couple months ago, OK? I want people to see it."

"Allllllriiiight" she said warningly. "It's gonna really show."

"Good!"

She wrapped a white plastic bib around my neck. Then she hoisted something that looked like a cross between a ray gun and and an electrician's drill. "This *is* gonna hurt, O.K.? You been warned. I'm not gonna bullshit you." As she spoke she pinched my lobe repeatedly. "How's that feel, honey, a little numb, huh? Is that number?"

"I still feel it."

"Now? Not number? How about now?"

"Yeah," I said

"Yeah?" she said.

But before I could answer, she hoisted the death ray to my lobe, slipped it between two metal teeth and pressed a button. With a sound like a hammer blow, steel shot through the meat of my ear and I yelped in pain. An instant later, the machine was holstered and Sandy was dabbing myear with cotton wool. In the mirror, I could see a lot of blood. "You're a bleeder," she said. "Oh, yeah, gosh, lookat dat. We got ourselves a bleeder here . . . ." My own reflected, paling face looked dazed.

"Lets put some of this on," she said, and the next thing I knew a wet dab of stinging fire sent me rocketing out of my chair as pure ethyl alcohol disinfected the open wound.

"Stay put," she said, shoving me back into my seat.

"Do women always go through this?" I gasped in disbelief.

"Honey, women got more balls than any man could ever imagine, OK? How do ya think we have babies? Whaddya think a man would do if they came along and said, 'we're gonna take a nine-pound baby outta your nuts? Huh? He wouldn't like that, would he? Hold still. I'm gonna put in the post."

"But I don't want—"

"Don't move!"

Painlessly, it was inserted. She screwed it very loosely. "It can't sit tight in there, understand? You gotta keep moving it around so that it dosen't heal with the metal in the skin. Otherwise, you'll be up shits creek and you'll have to come back for some unpleasant readjustment. Also, put alcohol on every day so it don't infect. If it infects, you'll be one sorry Van Gogh. Understood?"

"I understand," I said.

"And here's your precious crescent earring. First the post has to sit in there for a few days. Then you can start using this, OK? Lets have a look. You look great. A little too Jewish for Mick Jagger, in my opinion; more the Elvis type. I like Elvis."

"Well, I don't", I said, standing up. I dug into my jeans pocket, fished out fifteen dollars. "Thanks," I said.

"No problem. Send your friends."

Out I marched past the row of scrutinizing eyes on both sides of the counter. Behind me a voice called out: "You're cute!" and the place exploded with laughter.

When the door closed behind me, and I stood in the roaring noise and traffic of Fordham Road, I had to lower my blushing face a moment to orient myself. The dirty exhausted sunlight struck my already rattled nerves a glancing blow, as if to shame me for what I'd done. I stood there, defiant, scared, somewhat shocked, looking around me to see who'd notice the earring. No one seemed to care one way or another. I moved down the pavement a few yards, weaving between bodies among the tightly packed shopping crowds and turned my profile to them and stood still, ear offered for public examination. I noticed, now, a girl who reminded me a little of my ex-girlfriend Linda, snuck a glance at me, then looked away when I caught her curious eyes. This put a self-confidant smirk on my lips and I moseyed over to the window of a watchmaker's store and leaned up against the glass front, one boot raised behind me to the wall. Crossing my arms over my chest, à la the nameless Village street gypsy, I just stood there with an expression of inscrutable calm, as though I were not a tangled wormy mess of insecurities and fears but rather as wide-ranging, open and easy as the Western plains. And pretending to be so made me so, if only for a few minutes. I don't know whether anyone else was fooled, but I thought I spotted traces of doubt in the faces of a few passersby who couldn't seem to tell whether or not I was the thing I seemed to be. I really thought that if I fooled them, I could somehow fool myself.

"LOOK WHAT YOUR SON DID, GEORGE!" howled my mother when she saw it. The way she ran before me, hands clapped to cheeks, I could have been a Cossack on horseback entering her shtetl yard, sword in hand. My father emerged in his underwear, cigar poking from the side of his mouth, took one look and scowled. "Are you crazy? What did you *do?* You know what? This time you really did it! I'm telling you, I'm fed up with you. Do us a favor! Get the hell outta this house already, will you, and give us some peace already! You put an earring in your ear!? An earring! What the hell is wrong with you?"

"It's just an earring," I said.

"Oh, My God! Do you hear, George? *Just* an earring? You know that he can't get a Jewish burial because of that? They won't bury your own son! I blame you for this! I told you you should give it to him more often. You don't hit him enough! Now look what he did! He'll have to be buried with the Goyim!" She turned to me: "I disown you! Your father and I disown you! You're not our son anymore!"

"You *disown* me?" I turned to my father. "And you?"

"That's right, Mistah. You're disowned. Don't ask us for nuthing no more ever again!"

"ASK YOU?" I snapped "ASK YOU? For WHAT? What have you given me? What could you give me? You've got nothin' to give. Take your disownership and shove it!"

"Did you hear how he talks to us? Go, give him klep now. Be a man! BE A FATHER! Give it to him! Give him the belt in that stupid mouth of his! " She rushed up, reached to slap me and I batted away her hand. I glared at my father. "Go ahead. Take your best shot."

Shaking his head, he looked away tiredly and shuffled back into the bedroom, all his steam gone. Her I shoved past and stormed into my room. She followed me to the doorway, where she stood and said: "You broke your father's heart today! What made you do such a thing?"

But I was already packing. Pulling my meager wardrobe from the dresser and stuffing everything into a duffel bag, along with books, notebooks, and a poster of an Irish castle which I tore from the wall.

"I'm leaving!" I said. "It's over! I'm finished! I'm going, do you understand! Going! Forever! I have shot my wad in this place. I have suffered so much here, so much stupidity and intolerance, so much brutality and insanity, that I cannot bear to live here a single day more. Not a single minute! Do you understand me? I am going."

And I think that despite herself, something registered. She seemed, suddenly, against all odds, somehow to understand. Because of a sudden she stood quite still, watching. And for the first time in the history of that dingy room, with its pink walls and little cots that served as beds, the only sound was that of my own moving body as it prepared possessions for departure, her voice nowhere around. As though, in quieting herself, she quieted the entire apartment. And only at that moment was it real to me that indeed, this was it. As if I'd never had a moment's peace to really contemplate such a possibility. The taste of it was thrilling, but the thought of it was so wrenching that I began to cry a little. "That's right," I said, "I'm crying! So what? It's just nerves. Men cry, too! Men cry! Men like me who have lived through hell, we cry! And we are not ashamed! We are proud of crying! What haven't I experienced at your hands?! And at his hands in there! And don't you give me any of your Hitler did this to the Jews crap! You're *my* Hitler! What about what you did to *this* Jew, huh? Your own son!"

"Il est fou!" she said in that eerie, detached French-accented voice, speaking to herself.

"Yeah, I'm *fou*, alright. I'm real *fou!* But I'm outta here, at last! I'm going! But you should know that my heart is broken. That you didn't appreciate what a beautiful son you had! That you could have made me into something really wonderful instead of this wreck of lost dreams and fuse-blown nerves. I want you to know that I loved you *and* Pop *and* even that idiot brother of mine who's never around and never got hit or called names because that all went to me, didn't it! DIDN'T IT, you sick, sick woman! SIIIIICCCK-KKK!" I shrieked, all control lost now "YOU SICK, MENTALLY ILL CRAZY COCKSUCKING NUT!"

She just stood there. Didn't run to get a hangar or belt to beat me with, or shout for my father's reinforcement. She had grown very still, solemn, and looked different somehow. She even nodded as I wept my heart out, holding my pierced ear, which burned painfully, probably from all the blood rushing to my agitated head. I felt a savage headache coming on too. And when I looked up, my father had materialized by her side. He was wearing his trousers.

"We won't stop you," he said. "Maybe you're right. I don't know why we all don't get along, but we don't. It's too much for us. We can't handle you anymore."

"I'm not a horse! I'm not a *dog!* You didn't have to *handle* me. All you had to do was to *love* me like a parent loves a son. Instead, you treated me like a criminal. Like, like, like some kinda naked savage that needs to be kept behind bars for his own good. But I'm such a good person! That's what kills me, how good I am. *Not* the monster you made me out to be! *Not* the eternal problem child you got me labeled as in your own minds. I'm a good boy! A good boy!"

"You're not a boy anymore," she said coldly. "You're seventeen. When I was your age, I hid from the SS. It's time you learned to grow up."

"That's right, Mistah. You'll see what life is like on the other side of that door. Nobody's gonna put no food on your table. Nobody's gonna give you where to live or what to wear. You'll see."

The duffel bag was full and I fastened it closed. Then I walked past them to the hall closet, took out my peacoat and a black wool watch cap and put them on. Then I walked back to the bed, hoisted the duffel bag onto my shoulder and said, as if I were going to sea: "Well, it's time to be off. Don't ask where I'm going; I have no idea. Far away, though, I promise."

My mother looked at my father to see what he thought of my declaration. "George," she muttered, pulling at his t-shirt, "don't let your son go like that."

"Whaddya mean, don't let him go like that? He's a man. Let him go wherever the hell he wants. It's none of my business!"

"GEORGE," she said. "Please don't be crazy. Stop him."

"I'm not stopping nothing. You wanna go, you go, Mistah! But don't think you're coming back, understand?"

I understood.

> *Do us a favor! Get the hell outta this house already, will you, and give us some peace already! You put an earring in your ear!? An earring! What the hell is wrong with you?*

Plants at Work

Lynn McGee

Sunflowers bob on a raft near Chernobyl,
roots leaching atoms humming with intent
to harm, but diffusing like sugar in the slow
surge of some big flower's stalk,
its face tilting to follow the sun's arc,
working much harder than sunflowers I planted
in the backyard one summer, six lanky plants
framed by the kitchen window and mysteriously
snapped at the waist one day, my stepson
sulking, our weather toxic.

painting by Liz Kresch

Vladislav Khodasevich: Midlife Meltdown in Paris

Jenny Wade

During the unusually hot Parisian summer of 1924, 38-year-old Vladislav Khodasevich—regarded by Nabokov as the finest Russian poet since Blok—was suffering from an identity crisis. One of 3 million exiled from Soviet Russia, K. was spending days at a time lying in bed, looking up at the ceiling of his cheap one-room rental on the Boulevard Raspail: depressed, exhausted by insomnia, flat broke and without prospects. Just 2 years before he had been one of the brightest poets in Petersburg: the author of 3 acclaimed collections, with perhaps his greatest, "The Heavy Lyre," ready for print; compiling anthologies under the patronage of Maxim Gorky; reciting his verses at star-studded literary gatherings; delivering lectures on Pushkin; invited by the great poet Osip Mandelstam to join the Acmeists (K. declined); and granted a coveted apartment at the influential House of Arts.[1]

Russia's Silver Age was peaking, and K. was riding the wave. But in 1922 the ailing Blok was denied medical treatment by the Bolsheviks and died; K's friend and fellow poet Nikolay Gumilev was suddenly arrested and executed; and the leader of the new republic, V. Lenin, was busy preparing a long list of intellectuals soon to be forcibly deported[2]. K. saw what was coming and chose to leave. Bumping around Europe from Berlin to Prague, from Venice to Belfast, K. finally ran out of steam and dejectedly settled in Paris. Enduring poverty, illness, and the specter of obsolescence—what use is an émigré poet, cut off from his homeland, with an ever dwindling readership?—he offers us a slice of his tortured psyche in the poem "In Front of the Mirror."

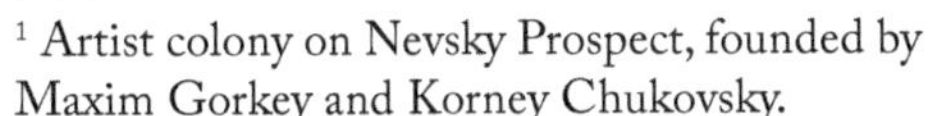

[1] Artist colony on Nevsky Prospect, founded by Maxim Gorkey and Korney Chukovsky.

[2] Khodosevich was unaware that he was also on this list. The discovery of this fact in the summer of 1924 made it clear that he could never return to his homeland and, moreover, that his work would never be published there again.

ПЕРЕД ЗЕРКАЛОМ

Nel mezzo del cammin di nostra vita.

Я, я, я. Что за дикое слово!
Неужели вон тот — это я?
Разве мама любила такого,
Желто-серого, полуседого
И всезнающего как змея?

Разве мальчик, в Останкине летом
Танцевавший на дачный балах,—
Это я, тот, кто каждым ответом
Желторотым внушает поэтам
Отвращение, злобу и страх?

Разве тот, кто в полночные споры
Всю мальчишечью вкладывал прыть,—
Это я, тот же самый, который
На трагические разговоры
Научился молчать и шутить?

Впрочем — так и всегда на средине
Рокового земного пути:
От ничтожной причины — к причине,
А глядишь — заплутался в пустыне,
И своих же следов не найти.

Да, меня не пантера прыжками
На парижский чердак загнала.
И Виргилия нет за плечами,—
Только есть Одиночество — в раме
Говорящего правду стекла.

18–23 июля 1924

IN FRONT OF THE MIRROR

Halfway through life's journey[1]

I, I, I. What a wild, elusive word!
Is that man over there really me?
Did mama really love someone like that?
With a pasty yellow face, half grey hair,
And all-knowing, like a snake?

The boy who danced at parties
At summer houses in Ostankino—[2]
Is that me? The one who's every remark
To a freshly hatched poet
Induces revulsion, malice and fear?

The one who laid his entire boyish energy
Into late night arguments—
Is that me? The very same one who
Has learned to keep quiet or make jokes
When talk turns to tragedy?

And still—it's always like this halfway
Along this earth's fateful path:
From one insignificant cause to another,
And look—you're lost in the wilderness,
And can't find your own tracks.

Yes, it was not a panther that
drove me with leaps to this Paris attic.
And Virgil is not at my shoulder.
There is only Loneliness—framed
In the looking glass, speaking the truth.

July 18–23, 1924, Paris

Thanks to Natasha Zhiltzova for her help with the translation.

---

[1] Dante, *The Inferno*

[2] A suburb of Moscow and the former estate of the fabulously wealthy Sherememtev family. In K's day, the land was subdivided into plots for country houses (dachas) and gardens for the middle class.

photographs by Gretchen Faust

Birds
Chemical

Chicago
Death

18
Education
Evolution

19
Excretion
Geometry

20
Geomorphic
Immunity

Two Poems

Rebecca Weiner Tompkins

AFTER YOU SAID I ALWAYS LOSE THINGS

The red birthstone fell
out of my ring, leaving
its crowned prongs empty,
a perfect chip chiseled
from my heart's bones.

I dreamed being stopped by
the long dark walkway
with bricked wall leading
to the locked iron gate enclosing
the fenced stairwell topped
by the steel door
beside sealed, heavy
draped windows, all
now forbidden.

The sweet, sharp birdsong
outside the room you loved
comes at me—
as it's surely been said before—
a barbed fist to the chest,
hooks and lodges in that space,
the lost ruby left.

SOUTHWESTERN

A man meets three
agents of death: lightning
nearly misses the tree; a
pale scorpion sits silent
at the door of his sleep; and
a truck swerves seconds
before it's head-on.
He begins to think
either God is calling him back
to that desert and he needs
to offer himself up, or it could
just be something else, even
nothing. Can one discern
what direction the signs are
pointing if one hates the
idea, the very word, plus
staring at the sun too long
has clouded one's vision?
The man talks it out
endlessly, to the wrong
listeners, shouts it in the
wrong rooms. Does God
want him whole or would he
rather make and take him
broken? What has already
been told: the lost get found
and darkness turns light and
sins can be turned around,
seems old; there's nothing
left to tell or teach. Now
this is where we might
leave him, find another
story, ours, which starts up
almost alike, only the names
or dates have been changed.
God, of course,
remains the same.

You Can Win: An Interview with Díre McCain

Edward S. Robinson

Díre McCain is a survivor. Editor-in-Chief at the internationally renowned *Paraphilia Magazine*, which has, since its inception in 2009, built a reputation for writing and art of outstanding quality while existing far beyond the realm of the mainstream, she's liked and respected in many underground circles. While she's contributed writing to a number of publications both on-line and in print, *Playing Chicken With Thanatos* is her first book-length work. It doesn't sit comfortably within the 'novel' category, nor is it a conventional autobiography or memoir. It is, however, Díre's story. By turns harrowing and hilarious, it's a consistently compelling read. I was keen to put some questions to Díre, and to find out if her achievements in recent years have happened because of, or in spite of, her difficult and often painful adolescence, the subject of *Playing Chicken With Thanatos*.

I began writing solely for therapeutic reasons, after emerging from a psychological coma induced by my refusal to come to terms with what I'd been through in my adolescence. At first, I was merely spewing memories and information onto the screen. As I went along, it became more of a purging, and ultimately developed a life of its own . . .

EDWARD S. ROBINSON: First, I'd like to say congratulations on an excellent book. The reception it's had has been very warm, and it seems to be reaching a fairly broad audience. How does that feel for you, as a writer, given the fact *Playing Chicken With Thanatos* is an intensely personal work?

DÍRE MCCAIN: Thank you! It feels incredible and oddly redemptive, since I misspent years trying to bury the chapter of my life on which the book focuses, inadvertently making myself unwell in the process. Fast forward to the present, and people are thanking me in beautiful, thoughtfully written emails for letting it all hang out. I can't begin to express how much that means. Not knowing if I had writing chops, self-doubt reared its crippling head throughout the creation process. Coupled with the personal nature of the book's content, I was apprehensive about releasing it right up until it was published. The fact that it's reaching, resonating and staying with people has made me realize that releasing it was the only choice.

ESR: You clearly had a quite unconventional upbringing that will doubtless prove to be quite an eye-opener for many readers. As you say yourself within the book, you were extremely keen—or perhaps desperate would be a more apposite choice of word—to escape that life, the situations and the people, so the idea of revisiting those formative years in such detail must have been extremely painful. What prompted you to write the book, and was it easier or more difficult than you had anticipated when you embarked on the project?

DM: I began writing solely for therapeutic reasons, after emerging from a psychological coma induced by my refusal to come to terms with what I'd been through in my adolescence. At first, I was merely spewing memories and information onto the screen. As I went along, it became more of a purging, and ultimately developed a life of its own, that of an actual book. Revisiting those years and reliving some of the events, although painful, was the only way those soul-decaying demons were ever going to be exorcised. It was difficult yet cathartic, as one would expect.

It was equally difficult much later in the process, after the foundation was built and I was struggling to complete the book as a writer rather than a person undergoing self-therapy.

ESR: In that sense, do you really feel it was a matter of choice? A lot of writers write through a kind of compulsion, and I recall an interview with Kathy Acker in which she said, "I write to get it out of me. I don't write to remember it." Would you say that was partly the case for you, with that sense of 'purging?'

DM: There was definitely a greater force at work. Even with the way the book began. I just woke up one day and felt impelled to write, as if I were possessed, after not writing a single word for ages. That compulsion then carried me through the near ten-year creation process, even when I felt like throwing in the towel or worse yet, trashing the entire work in progress, which nearly happened more than once. Thank god I ignored that mad impulse.

ESR: From beginning to end, how long did the book take to complete?

DM: The first words were banged out in spring of 2004, and the final draft was completed in autumn of 2013, with the book being published on November 14, 2013. I never anticipated it taking that long, but various distractions kept getting in the way, and the nature of the book is such that it couldn't have been forced, rushed, or done half-heartedly.

ESR: In many respects, of course, the underlying narrative, the story, was already set, being determined by real-life events. How much did you, as an author, have to 'intervene' in order to render the sequence within the book coherent?

DM: Well, the book began as a series of what could have been standalone stories, aside from the

photograph of Díre McCain by David George

beginning and ending chapters. As it continued to mushroom and assume the form of a book, I realized that there needed to be some kind of continuity, although not necessarily linear, since life is rarely linear. Two or three drafts into it, I did some rearranging and created segues between the chapters, and voila!

Also, there was a surplus of material going in and coming out, since my adolescence was unrelentingly eventful. I had to decide what and who to include. Narrow it down, that is. I probably could have written a 1000-pager, if I'd told the whole tale.

ESR: The narrative is straightforward, direct, but without being in any way 'dumbed down' or overtly populist, and there's a very definite rhythm to the

DM: Not much at all, due to the kind of book it is. With the earliest draft, I simply let it all spill out of my head, as if the computer were a passenger stuck next to me on an interminable flight, and in some places, a narcoleptic shrink. Many people have remarked on the conversational nature, saying it feels as though I'm speaking to them directly, which I was hoping to achieve.

In the beginning, I was also re-teaching myself how to write, having not only removed myself from higher education a few years prior, but life as well. My brain was rusty, although I think that was a blessing in that I wasn't bogged down by the usual crap writers worry about, including an audience. I simply wanted to get the story out of my head and onto the screen. When I did begin to edit, it was mostly for stylistic and structural purposes, so the readers would remain interested and unconfused.

Now, my fiction is an entirely different animal that does indeed exist on the fringes. It requires a turn of mind that was absent in *Playing Chicken With Thanatos,* although I still think it's entirely accessible, albeit bound to offend certain people.

prose and a strong sense of structure overall. How much editing did it take to achieve that balance between accessibility and remaining true to yourself, as someone with what one might call more 'fringe' literary tastes?

ESR: On the subject of your literary tastes, you are perhaps best known as the editor in chief at *Paraphilia Magazine*. How did the work with the publication inform the writing process? Do you think it's helped connect you to an audience for the book?

DM: I'm a lifelong habitual reader, but my peculiar and often uncooperative brain requires complete focus when in writing mode. I can't have my head swarming with other people's words, no matter how remarkable. It's like having those people in the room with me, reading their work aloud while I'm trying to write. Even emails and texts can clutter and distract. As a result, *Paraphilia* became a persistent albeit unintentional hindrance to the writing process. Every time I attempted to return to my book, the magazine would intervene, making it impossible. Although I was aware it was happening, I didn't realize the true magnitude until I put *Paraphilia* on the backburner and began focusing on my own work.

Paraphilia *became a persistent albeit unintentional hindrance to the writing process. Every time I attempted to return to my book, the magazine would intervene, making it impossible. Although I was aware it was happening, I didn't realize the true magnitude until I put* Paraphilia *on the backburner and began focusing on my own work.*

On the upside, I'm sure the magazine did connect me to an audience for the book, although I have no way of knowing to what degree. It certainly connected me with some extraordinary and insanely talented human beings, many of whom I now consider family.

ESR: The book's published by Apophenia, which is part of the *Paraphilia* setup. Is this indicative of a particularly antagonistic stance to the conventional publishing model, in eschewing conventional publishing channels? If so, what are your reasons?

DM: No, it's not that elaborate, and I don't have any real issues with conventional publishing, since I've never attempted to go that route. I'd be opining about a subject I'm experientially unfamiliar with there. That said, it's common knowledge that obscure and lesser-known artists in any field are often treated differently than those with a name, and the almighty dollar usually dictates the course, as with any business.

Apophenia was created to provide a home for some of the *Paraphilia Books* titles, after that label was killed last year. It seemed logical to publish my own book as well, especially given its subject matter. That decision was reinforced by my memories of an experience I had in 2006, when I consulted briefly with some industry folks, long before the book was even close to being complete. I immediately realized that if I followed their advice, *Playing Chicken With Thanatos* would never come to life in its envisioned and intended form. I'm certain a hatchet would've been taken to it in a number of places, followed by lettered yet uninitiated people attempting to rewrite portions of a story they've never lived and have no right to tell.

Of course, I want people to read the book, and had an established publisher come along with an offer that was agreeable in terms of creative control, I would've jumped on it. Primarily because I wouldn't be flying solo in letting the world know that the book exists. PR can be a real slog when you have no budget to hire anyone and don't know anyone who works for any major media outlets. I'm relying largely upon word of mouth, and have been fortunate that some wonderful people at independent venues have generously offered a helping hand.

ESR: It's fair to say then that by some margin you value artistic integrity and control over financial reward. Do you think art (in any form) and business (big-money or otherwise) are fundamentally incompatible bedfellows?

DM: I don't think they're incompatible by nature. As with much else that's completely illogical in our world, that conflict is human-made and deliberate. I believe that if the people in charge and society at large pulled their indoctrinated heads out of their rigidly conventional asses, a healthy balance between art and business could be found and sustained on a grand scale. Humankind would be better off for it as well.

All of the characters and events are real, but who wants to read a monotonic Joe Fridayesque account? I believe the trick to telling a good true story is to make it as engaging as possible without compromising the facts.

Back to the first part of your question: I may not be as adamant about other works of mine, but artistic integrity and control were indispensible with *Playing Chicken With Thanatos*. The book represents a significant and defining chunk of my life. Not only having lived the experiences chronicled, but the blood, sweat, tears, and years that went into writing about it as well.

ESR: A number of reviews have drawn comparisons between *Playing Chicken With Thanatos* and a number of other works, including Bukowski's novels and *You Can't Win* by Jack Black, which was a great influence on William S. Burroughs, and I understand you haven't (yet) read. I would also locate the book in a broader and also much older tradition, that of the picaresque novel, on account of its episodic approach to narrative. Where do you yourself see *Playing Chicken With Thanatos* sitting in stylistic, literary terms?

DM: I see *Playing Chicken With Thanatos* sitting in its own unique place. That's why the BISAC code is Non-Classifiable, and I refer to the book as a book or work of literature, rather than a memoir, novel, or any other specific label. I'm probably doing myself a disservice in terms of marketing, but my aversion to categorization and the pigeon-holing, thought-swaying baggage that comes with it is at an all-time high.

Having said all that, the book is definitely autobiographical. The only fictional aspects are set forth in the thoughtfully worded disclaimer on the copyright page, which everyone should read before embarking on the journey. All of the characters and events are real, but who wants to read a monotonic Joe Friday-esque account? I believe the trick to telling a good true story is to make it as engaging as possible without compromising the facts. It did help tremendously that the people in my life at that time were real characters, as in eccentrics, who pretty much wrote themselves. Plus, as I already mentioned, there was no shortage of material, a fact that influenced my decision to go with an episodic structure. Add my often maddening exceptional memory, the emotional element, my voluble nature and personality as a whole, and you have what became the book's style.

And *You Can't Win* has been at the top of my reading list for a couple of months now. As soon as I complete the handful of writing projects I'm currently working on, I plan to jump in.

ESR: Who are the writers and indeed, artists more broadly, you would align yourself with?

DM: Visionaries, genuine mavericks, and anyone with an artistic fire inside that refuses to be extinguished, despite repeated attempts by external forces.

ESR: You're obviously someone who's passionate about music as well, although *Playing Chicken With Thanatos* is, to my mind, a book that doesn't tie itself to its time by referencing music too heavily. What would be the book's soundtrack, if it were to have one?

DM: Interesting you mentioned that, because I do have an ever growing, ever changing soundtrack in my head, should the book ever become a film or television series. Similar to my present-day life soundtrack, it could never be shackled to a single time, and would include an eclectic and encompassing variety of music from the 1920s through the 1990s, with a splash from the Classical era as well.

ESR: It would definitely work as a film, because it's plot-driven and character-based—which life rarely is (beyond the fact that everyone is the lead character in the film of their own life). In your dream scenario, who would direct a film version of *Playing Chicken With Thanatos*, and who would play you?

DM: Overambitious perhaps, but I'd love to co-direct it myself, along with a (tel)empathic [sic] and necessarily skilled accomplice who'd do the story justice, since it's an arena in which I'm inexperienced. As for the casting, I believe most of the actors, including whoever would play me, have yet to be discovered. They're probably performing in unsung theatres somewhere, or in truly independent films. As a theatre student and aspiring actor in early adulthood, that's where I encountered some of the most phenomenal talent, hands down.

On a related note, the prospect of adapting the story into a film or television series was discussed with those industry folks I mentioned earlier. They claimed that no one in Hollywood would go near it, since it involves underage kids engaging in illicit activities. Which, of course, never happens in the real world, right? More important, the aspects of the story that could be deemed controversial are incidental to the big picture, which I believe has broad appeal. It wouldn't be a Larry Clark film, far from it. There are a number of themes and undercurrents at work in *Playing Chicken With Thanatos* that transcend the obvious or potentially shocking. One doesn't need to be a junkie or juvenile delinquent to relate, and I think anyone who's read the book would agree. Although there are certainly dissimilarities, the idea that kids are a different species than adults is beyond ridiculous. I rarely quote others, but Robert Seitz (who interviewed the author earlier in the year) summed it up so clearly and eloquently here:

"There is a desire to flesh out the experiences of a troubled youth in a way that avoids the pedantic, and gives credibility to the awareness and individuality of youth, making the book something that should interest anyone struggling with the impositions of our uniform, mediated modernity. It is medicine, the kind that's delivered with shock paddles."

ESR: It's one of the most well-worn clichés that everyone has a book in them—albeit one I personally don't adhere to. Is *Playing Chicken With Thanatos* your one book, or do you feel that having made the initial breakthrough, there's more to come?

DM: I have no plans to compose another autobiographical book, and probably don't have another 350-pager in me either, but who knows? Assuming I reach the average life expectancy, I still have several decades ahead of me and am only getting warmed up on the creative front. I returned to SoCal in 2006 to focus on my creative endeavors, including writing, and have yet to give it my all. Back to *Paraphilia,* a project that began as an unplanned leap in the dark, for lack of a better description. It's been life-changing and emotionally rewarding, and will continue indefinitely, although not at the same level of intensity as the past five years. I feel I've done what I needed to there, and it's time to move forward and tend to myself again. The magazine is finally in a position where it's operating somewhat independently and not eating a significant chunk of my life, which means I can focus on my own work for the foreseeable future. There are currently a handful of projects in progress that will come to life in the coming months.

Kimberly, photograph by Ruby Ray

Atomic Submarine

Marc Olmsted

We kissed while *Atomic Submarine* blazed in the TV midnight, an old childhood spooky thriller that was still rather disturbing. A submarine rams this flying saucer and weird sexual goo comes out, in stark black and white, and a gooey one-eyed tentacled alien (like a devil-god) lures the crew members away; one gets cooked by electricity, blinking in negative, while another has a space hatch close on him like a scythe. Saw that on LA's "Chiller" TV as a disturbed 8-year-old, and it was still rather creepy in that '50s sleazy way, rattling the subconscious with perverse images, Eisenhower's Id. But Nicki! Catgirl! Nymphet ex-teen junkie, now just 21, baby-faced baby doll, conversant in all my literary heroes. Little cigarette smoker, hair jet black thatch with a splotch of purple, two braids hanging down (I had wanted to kiss those braids at first sight), little kitten, a sort of teen Siouxie-Sioux, marvelous white tight little body. "I think my butt's too big," ah, insane these women and their butts, when Nicki had the cutest heartshaped butt of all time. "I have this thing for writers." O honey!

> *A submarine rams this flying saucer and weird sexual goo comes out, in stark black-and-white, and a gooey one-eyed tentacled alien (like a devil-god) lures the crew members away; one gets cooked by electricity, blinking in negative, another has a space hatch close on him like a scythe.*

Nicki, scary, impossible to hold, anything could happen like Texas dynamite, I kissed her thigh in my mind, her ankle dainty on the sheet, her little toes, I thought of her earnest fascination with the world, she had come from a pit full of horrors even I hadn't seen, "slamming dope on Skid Row," poor little eyes fogged with dope, o heartbreak, o bleat, o lamb.

Too much! Too heavy! Stop the jukebox! Finish the horror movie! No black valentines! Surrender to the impossible world of doom and honey!

After digging my thumbs into my neck, I drove to an AA meeting weeping in the car, afraid, but the fear had found its sorrow of teary release, and my neck softened as I wept behind sunglasses in the LA sunblast of a 1987 rush hour.

Then a call on the answering machine from Nicki when I got in, stepping from the foggy streets of Venice Beach where the yellow moon fulled its yellowy mouth in a blear. So I called her and she said "I wish I could see you now," and I glanced at the clock. *I'd be asleep by now,* ordinarily, workhorse, but I said, "Why don't you come over?" and she raced in the moonlight, and we pounded the sheets, o nipple biter, of muscular taut cunt and tiny bud clit, sex! sex! sex! such a hot little fuck as she whispered appreciations up at me after my ego had taken such a beating from this town of hell. So I stumbled into work, neck loose, goon grin, planning to see her again next night, suck her lips, of face and ass, hold her little breasts in the beat-up world.

But then I had a Nicki headache because I was afraid of Nicki—she might be a vampire—she might be a pony that would run away—a young mustang filly that would run and her hooves would sound in my aching head—she might be Bathsheba going to bed as she did with arms of bracelets clanging as we fucked—she might be poison—she might be a bottle with an X, with three X's!—she might be a needle contaminated with AIDS—I had a Nicki headache because she wouldn't call—now she called and I still had a Nicki headache.

She came over, started acting weird and finally said it was all too new, she was worried, she'd never been intimate before with anyone "even coherent," she was afraid of hurting me, she was afraid, and though she undressed, and was in my bed in just bra and panties, she got up, dressed and left like Garbo. "I'll call you Saturday or Sunday."

—the heroin girl—now appearing in your living room—now calling into your telephone—now vanishing with withdrawal symptoms—the heroin girl gives a party and you're invited—you're the guest of honor—you are the only guest—and the heroin girl whispers—she says—"you're the one"—

an excerpt from Wild Kingdom

photograph of Allen Ginsberg in Tompkins Square Park, NYC, 1967 by Charles Gatewood

Afro-Surreal Excerpt

D. Scot Miller

Let me tell you how I met Sham Black.

West Virginia, Dunbar Jr. High School football field, 123rd Annual Commode Bowl, Riverside Rats versus The Hillside Rams.

Every Thanksgiving morning the men of Dunbar, on both sides of the railroad tracks that split through the town (Riverside and Hillside) begin to drink. At ten o'clock, they stagger into their F-1 s, Monte Carlos, and Firebirds ("Quality car there, buddy!"), and honk their horns in a slow, drunken parade down Dunbar Avenue, cold beer in hand, until they reach the football field at the end of town near the river. Then they soak the field until it's nothing but a mud pool. Then they get drunk. Then they try to play football. I was sitting at the top of the bleachers nursing my father's flask for a pre-supper buzz.

". . ." this black guy in a leather peacoat and blue and white wool hat said from the top of the bleachers.

"Pardon me?" He motioned me up to where he was sitting. I went up.

"They're doing a version of an ancient ritual. Early agricultural tribes had orgies in the fields right before planting. It was supposed to be good for both the crops and the tribe. Been around for thousands of years."

"Who are you, Mr. Wizard? Looks like a bunch of drunk rednecks rolling in the mud to me."

"Just because they don't know they do it don't mean they ain't doing it. I've a feeling that somebody back 100 years ago knew. See that guy over there?"

He pointed to "Big" John Gillaspell, town paralytic, who had just taken off his mud-covered shirt and was spinning it around over his head like a helicopter blade. His sagging basketball shorts were caked to black, and contrasted starkly with the fish-belly paleness of the fifteen pounds of flaccid flab flapping and swaying side to side in his drunken victory stumble upfield.

"Whoooooooo!" Big John wailed until a ball of phlegm choked him to a silent hobbit-like trot.

"That guy and his good wife are going to go home tonight full of beer and hubris. He is not going to bathe and she's not going to ask him to. They're going to put on their favorite soul album and they're going to roll around in the all that dirt and mud. They're going to fuck—"

I laughed. "No," I said with a guffaw, loud and drunken.

"They're going to fuck like they haven't in 364 days. And tomorrow morning, they'll feel cleaner, stronger and clearer than they have since last year, without shame, long before they've showered and changed the sheets. And come the next harvest cycle a new crop of football players and plant workers will be born, with a healthy green field to play, drink, and fuck on. It's been that way for a long, long time. There's a lot going on behind the veil."

I took another sip from my flask and let the Rapid Cur warm away the chill. I liked the way he talked. I wanted to talk like that one day. With the words just coming out like that and shit. I would have definitely talked more if I could have talked like that back then.

"Pez?"

"Yeah, thanks. Yo, man, what is that?!"

"Tupac Pez Dispenser. You don't get these?"

"That is so dope! Hell, no."

"They got Biggie, too. Want another one?"

"Thanks. That is too ill."

"Been making them for nearly twenty years where I'm from."

"Where you from?"

"Knot Frum Hear."

"I know that. But where you from?"

He just smiled at me. "Hey, you smoke la?"

"Huh?"

"Herbs. You indulge in sacred herbs?"

"Naw, man. And I don't know nobody either."

"I'm not looking. I'm saying I got smoke." He

pulled out a fat joint and lit it right there. At the top of the bleachers. In front of everybody.

"What are you doing?!" I started to get up. It was the stinkiest pot I'd ever smelled in my life. Smelt like someone was brewing a batch of skunk tea.

"The cops are right there, man. You're on your own partner. I don't even know you."

"It's cool man, this ain't weed, frop." He coughed. "Look." He blew a cloud of smoke in the direction of the cluster of plaid parka-wearing Wall Mall shoppers. They didn't even turn their heads. Cautiously, I watched him collect another cloud of thick gray smoke in his cheeks and expel it, where it hung heavily and deliberately over the crowd.

Before you take a hit, understand this: Only I am nobody. You are somebody. They are everybody else. That's your nature, their nature and my preference... You are somebody, not nobody and damn sure ain't everybody. You are Myself. See what I'm saying?

"Besides, nobody round here would have the imagination to do this. You cats still smoking dirt out this way, this isn't anywhere near weed to these people. Wouldn't be nothing to you if I hadn't of told you. And nobody smokes weed in the bleachers, right? So, I'm nobody right now. Get it? Have a seat, little brother, and hit this." I reached for it. Handing it over, he let me get the sticky cigarette to my lips.

"Before you take a hit, understand this: Only I am nobody. You are somebody. They are everybody else. That's your nature, their nature and my preference. I repeat, you are not nobody or everybody, so you will not do the things that nobody does or the things that everybody does. Rather, you will do the things that nobody does not do and not everything that everybody does. You are somebody, not nobody and damn sure ain't everybody. You are Myself. See what I'm saying? How does the old saying go? I find Myself, mate, generate, gestate, huh, Myself, birth from the hearth, Myself. See?"

"You're saying I am somebody."

"Say it!"

"I AM—"

"Say it!"

"SOMEBODY!"

"Yes!"

We both laughed and I took a deep pull of the joint and began to cough immediately. They were deep, deep coughs that seemed to start in my stomach and wrench through my lungs. I couldn't catch my, catch my, breath. And, and, I felt my throat constrict as my tongue strained from mouth, mouth, my mouth. Spittle and snot sprayed from every hole in my head, my head. I gagged, gagged, gagged, gagged, and emptied the contents of my stomach through the slats through the below my feet onto the gravel below through the slats . . . .

"See," he said, rubbing my back. "You were thinking you were nobody. You are somebody, only I am nobody. For you, hitting that like me made you sick. Nobody smokes like me. Work with nobody and everybody will never know. If you want to be somebody, remember that."

"Who are you, fuck, man, man?"

"Sham, Black, Black Sham Black." He extended his leather-clad arm, stuck out his hand, still wearing that smile. I shook it, trying to get a glimpse of his tattoo.

"Hey, scene seen one won of these deez before for?" He held out his forearm. The tattoo was the outline of a black heart. The crowns curved slightly into curlicues at the top with roots forming a base at

photograph by Kym Ghee

the bottom.

"Yeah, Janet Jackson's got one on her ass."

"It's on her back, but butt you ewe seen it be four right write?"

"Yeah."

"How many thymes?"

"Shit, I don't know. A couple dozen."

"No whut it is?"

"It is what it is. Nope."

"It's a Sankofa. An Adinkra symbol from the ancient language of the Akan people of Ghana. It means 'Go back and fetch it.' Means go back and reclaim the past passed, dig? Get the essence of the culture's knowledge and wisdom and use it as a tool for the future. How many times you seen it?"

"I would say, excluding ogling the Velvet Rope, four. But I've heard that word before. How you say it?"

"Sankofa."

"Yeah, I've heard that word before somewhere. Man that's some good shit. Got me all paranoid. That word scares the shit out of me."

"There's a reason for that. Great horrors were done to the place and the people to put that kind of poison into the Word word. Sankofa. Look it up, millions of people were slaughtered in and around the word the Word so you'll get psychically ill eel when you here it. Isn't that fucked up? This," he pointed at his tattoo, "came first. But when eye say the Word you don't hear 'go back and fetch it' here, you see images of the holocaust. Which would discourage you from going back and fetching it, even if ewe new, huh? Why would somebody want to do that?"

"Could be a coincidence."

"No, it wasn't."

"You like my pops, huh? He doesn't believe in coincidences either."

"I believe in coincidences, just that they can be planned."

"What the fuck that mean?"

"Living without a creation myth contributes to the subtle but pervasive quality of disorientation in modem life as anomie: the sense of not fitting in, which is an inescapable condition of those who have no conception of what they are supposed to fit into. That's about alienation. I red it in a book called Maps of Time by a scientist named David Christian. You reed?"

"Well, yeah."

"You seemed ashamed that you read."

"I'm not ashamed of shit, man." I went to take another sip when I realized that I didn't need it. I was higher than giraffe pussy.

"Ever read *Fahrenheit 451?*"

"Bradbury, sure."

"What if someone thought that instead of getting rid of the books, getting rid of the readers would be more cost-effective? Readers write books, right? These daze with all the word processors and voice-activated pages."

"I never heard of that," I say.

"It's knew. You can speak into a mic and the words just print out on the page."

"Cool."

"Yeah, but writing is going to get easier and easier. There are going to be more and more books out there, more than ever before. Too many! Too many books, can you believe it? So many books coming so fast that you can't tell what's enriching and what's draining you, making you tired. The hard thing is going be the reading. Remembering what we do it for, you know?"

"Yeah." I looked up at him. I did know what he meant. I really knew. For a second, it was like we were in a vacuum and it was just me and him. I really looked at him. He looked like a hairy version of my dad. Strong jaw, covered in a trimmed beard, smiling at me. This nigga loved me. Loved me in such a way that I'd never felt before or since. It wasn't a sexual thing or anything like that. It was some deep shit, like the kind of love you get for someone after being pinned down in some shit together, but deeper. That's what I saw in those eyes, when I felt what he meant when he said "reading."

He stood and stretched.

"Well youngblood, nice meeting you." He was about to leave me, stoned, on the bleachers thinking about these mud-covered puds having hot, brown love.

I remember seeing the orgy taking place before my eyes. The muddy, breasted men rolling over each other in a slick tangle for the ball. Their wives and children screeching from the sides in a frenzied Bacchanal. The center bending, the QB mounting, and the clashing of wet muddy flesh beginning anew. Satyrs and nymphs poking, licking, prodding, grunting like pigs, braying like mules, barking, wailing, in the mud, officiated by Ted from the Stop and Shop who provided the kegs and his own whistle.

"OK, Sham. See you around?" I wanted to tell him that I noticed that all of the players were semi-erect, but what the fuck would that have sounded like?

"Probably not. Say, do you swim?"

"Doggy paddle."

"Not good enough. Living off a river like this, you could really learn how to swim."

"Sounds good." It did.

"All soul. All feet." And he walked off the bleachers and out of Dunbar forever.

America as Afterimage in True Detective

Marian St. Laurent

THE MORAL RIGHTEOUSNESS OF THE Western genre with its clear definitions of good vs. evil looks quaint from where we find ourselves in 2014. If heroes are symbols of evolving cultural values, the fact that our pantheon is a line up of likeable "terrorists," criminals and sleeper agents indicates a national identity in crisis. In this Brave New World where bad is the new good, con artists restore faith in the American dream while PTSD-wracked detectives are today's guardians of order.

The rise of The Southern: film and television representations of Louisiana or the Deep South.

Out of the contradictions and uncertainties of the American situation, the "Southern" has emerged as the "Western" of our time. Ambient and immersive treatments of the historically and geographically baroque South provide a metaphorical space for audiences to contemplate the twin ghost-worlds of our preindustrial past and post-industrial present.

Republic vs. Empire

True Detective engages the symbolism of the Deep South by leveraging the neglected infrastructure and environmental collapse of contemporary Louisiana for its aesthetic language, tonality and plot. From title design onward, the landscape and the ubiquitous oil refineries have dramatic significance on a par with the show's protagonists as a nonverbal means by which contesting visions of American-ness are

VISIONS OF AMERICA IN TRUE DETECTIVE

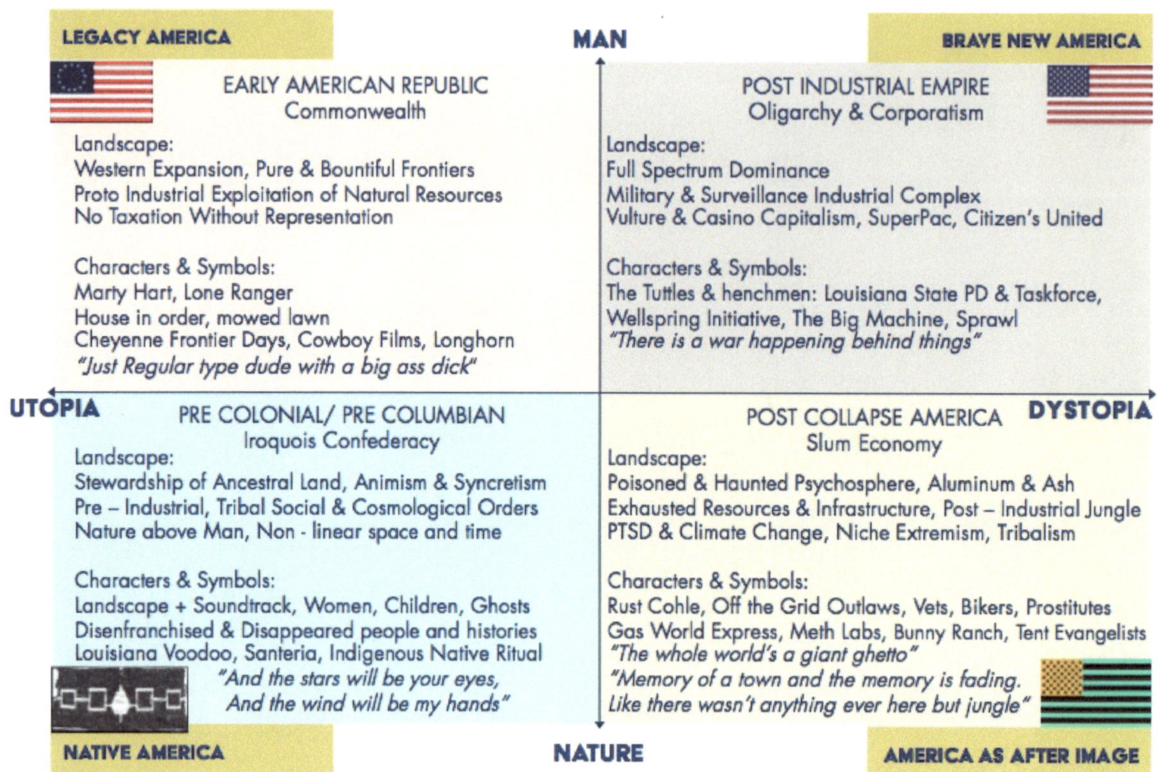

Contesting visions of America in *True Detective*.

played out against each other.

Immersive and dramatic aerial shots of the Louisiana bayou are a counterpoint to the heady, philosophical dialectic between Marty and Rust. The borderline between the suburbs and the swamp highlights how fine the line is between civilization and wilderness, directing our attention toward the point at which domesticity ends and ferality begins.

The fine line between wilderness and civilization.

Marty Hart is surrounded by the symbols of Legacy America. As a caricature of the "Lone Ranger," he embodies the values of the Early American Republic with his salt of the earth faith in boundaries, community, and "decency." In Marty's worldview, everything has its place. As a self-described "regular guy with a big-ass dick," he even frames marital infidelity as having a role in maintaining the order of his

"Illegal business controls America."—Boogie Down Productions (Strip club/oil refinery title montage)

family life. When he gets home from work, he puts his keys in the same spot. He's territorial—he "likes mowing his own lawn."

Marty is a "people person," a domesticated frontiersman & guardian of social order, even after his personal world collapses. When he leaves the Louisiana State PD to start his own small business, "Hart Investigative Solutions," the singular decorative addition to the office is a "Cheyenne Frontier Days" poster. In the years after his divorce, he eats TV dinners while watching cowboy movies. When he reunites with Rust to repay their "debt" and focus on solving the case together, he speaks on behalf of Legacy America when he confides, "you end up becomin' somethin' you never intended. I guess you never even really know why."

America as Afterimage

"This place is like somebody's memory of a town and the memory is fading. Looks like there wasn't anything here but jungle."

Wilderness is a constant threat to order in *True Detective*. Neglected weeds grow between the cracks, along deserted freeways and in the broken pavement of abandoned parking lots. Orphaned bikes rust away in indeterminate piles of litter as the whole rotten post-hurricane mess melts into a lush overgrowth that swallows up traces of a civilization that once was. As if to flaunt the victory of chaos over order, the weeds show America as a forgotten afterimage of itself and reveals it for the "jungle" it has become and was before.

Rust Cohle is the nocturnal opposite of Marty, a symbol of the deterioration and chaos of post-collapse America. In Rust's worldview, the American Dream was only ever a ghost. Marty describes Cohle's "rawboned" ferality by telling the detectives it "took three months to get him over to the house for dinner." Off the grid and without a television or a family, Rust doesn't recognize institutional order ("Who the fuck's Eddy?") or the myth of progress ("Time is a flat circle"). His home is Spartan, bereft of the domestic trappings of the American dream and its accompanying melodramatic distractions. Abandoned by his mother, raised by a Vietnam vet, and having lost the daughter and wife he had, Cohle's life as "a cycle of violence and degradation" endows him with a "real mind" for the case.

Pre and post collapse visions of America—top: Marty's Legacy America. "I like mowing my own lawn," " vs. bottom: "This your place?" / "It's my lease." A feral living room at the Bunny ranch presents the slum economy waiting at the end of the American Dream.

Rust begins the six-minute tracking shot of the stash house heist by feeling his pulse. The south Texas ghetto scene unfolds in the single shooter gaming aesthetics of *Call of Duty,* implicitly reframing conventions of the Western shootout with cinematic vocabulary of 21st-century warfare. As rogue cop disguised as outlaw disguised as cop, Rust taps into a natural order overriding a parade of illusions. His language devolves into a primal growl as he rides the rising violence in a flow state.

It is only through the hallucinogenic lens of PTSD and synesthesia that Rust can clearly read through the cognitive dissonance of corporate brand-speak (The "Wellspring Initiative") and see it for what it really is in order to track corruption's "sprawl." By using instinct to "read the signs" across the "aluminum and ash" bayou where "nothing grows in the right direction," Rust maintains a "meta" relationship with social order to subvert and survive it. From his place outside and between, he is uniquely suited to decode the double-speak of institutional power (The Tuttles, Louisiana State Police Department and the taskforce) and negotiate the terrain of outlaw life (Iron Crusaders, Gas World Express, and drug cartels).

Dystopian, Post-Collapse America is marked by a new kind of tribalism and "niche extremism" that requires both pre-industrial survival skills like bow hunting, as well as modern military training. Rust's hypersensitivity endows him with the ability to see beyond things, to "mainline the secret truth of the universe." His relationship to the "psychosphere" connects him with the cosmological mappings of a pre-colonial landscape.

The landscape as symbol of the disappeared and disenfranchised.

Precolonial America – Do You Believe In Ghosts?

Children signify the future as they convey generational, long-view thinking. The disappearance of women and children in *True Detective* is tantamount to an end for humanity. The surviving family members of victims are speechless and broken. Trauma, grief and addiction has stopped time for them. They wear their trauma and live half-lives, paralyzed by "cerebral events" and crippled by migraines from mysterious chemicals.

Immersive aerial views of sugar cane fields, cypress groves, and lush jungle are presented from above or in tracking shots and transitions that draw visceral connections between the physical degradation and disappearance of the bayou communities and the ubiquitous presence of oil refineries. In Episode 2, we cut from Ms. Kelly bending over in pain from "headaches that come on like storms" and close ups of her chemically damaged nails to an aerial view of the bayou. The tattered bayou, like the violated bodies of ritual murder victims is "cut up like a jigsaw" by oil pipelines and refineries, doomed to disappear like the voiceless "unsolveds" whose records are "filed in error" and don't get press.

Pipelines covering up this coast like a jigsaw. Place is gonna be under water in 30 years.

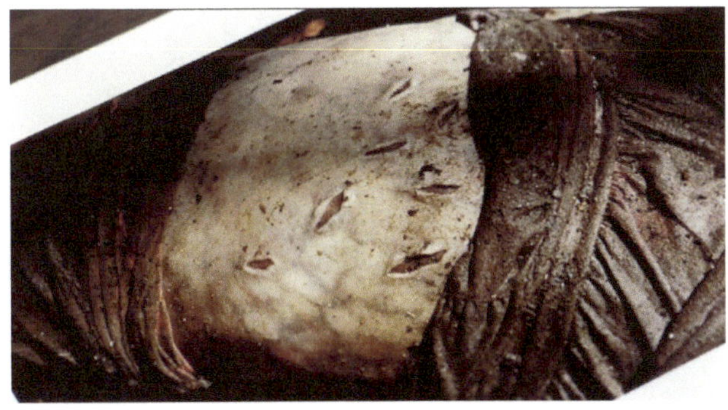

As a silent witness to atrocity, the landscape becomes the voice of the disappeared, which Rust is able to decipher by listening to other sensorial input ignored by Enlightment prejudice toward visible, observed, reality. By hearing color and tasting sound, he takes guidance from cosmological and metaphysical orders to read the signs of the exhausted, poisoned landscape. The landscape reminds us through its accompanying soundtrack of judgment and redemption, what is "owed by our society for our mutual illusions."

Louisiana's not-land/not-water landscape becomes a shattered mirror to project our disappearing future onto. The landscape speaks sensorially, through a soundtrack of slave songs, indigenous symbols, talisman and rituals—traces of cultures and practices disappeared by genocidal economies of the Antebellum South and Western Expansion. When Rust notices a billboard for missing children that reads "Who Killed Me?" the voice of our future and our past speaks simultaneously.

The Detective's Curse

"It was a horrible, horrible thing. We saw it on TV—what we're in the clutches of and I prayed and prayed for that [woman's] family- and its me, its me."

"Sprawl" is a symbol of the omnipresence of corporate influence in today's Brave New America. The full-spectrum dominance of the Tuttle family tree—their involvement in "a lot of different things" reaching from the police department to the news media—is an oblique reference to the Prism-riddled, crony capitalism of Empire. "How about we track all the missing persons within ten miles of every Walmart? In fact, why don't we go after Sam Walmart?, the police chief facetiously asks before dismissing Rust for insubordination.

This sprawling "family tree" is marked on the one hand by the ubiquitous presence of menacing oil refineries, and on the other by the conspicuous absence of evidence for the dead and missing women and children disappearing across bayou country.

According to Marty, "The Detective's Curse" is the inability of a detective to read signs right under his nose because he's following the wrong clues.

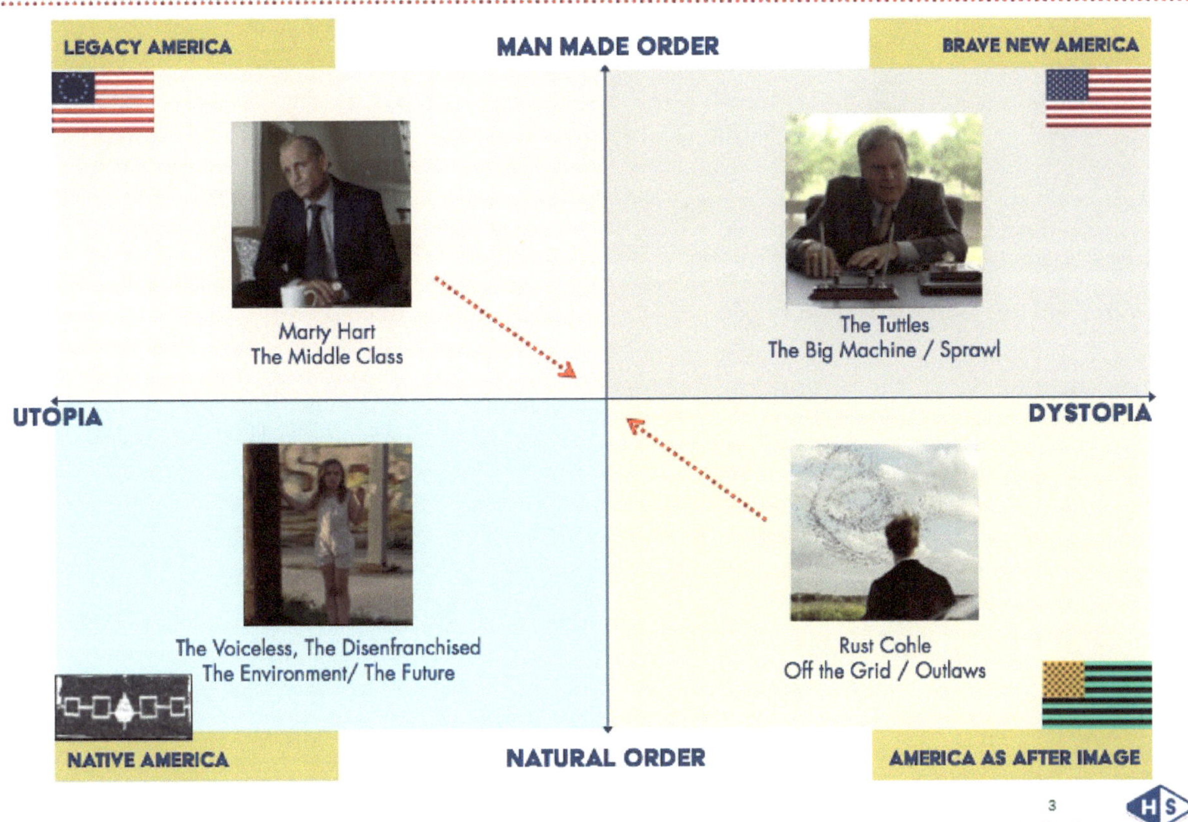

How light won over darkness.

Metaphors of veils, illusions, and blindness, are woven throughout the series. "We're in a muddy swamp here and the alligators are swimming all around us . . . we don't see em," says Rust. The hubris of consumerism and its looming debt has made "everybody think they gonna be somebody that they not" and "like a lot of dreams, there's a monster at the end of it."

"Without me there is no you"

Marty works within the system and then steps out of it, closer toward Rust. Rust, in his older age opens up toward Marty. The intimacy and power of their union toward a single-minded cause not only makes good storytelling, but is also good political strategy. As symbols of contrasting worldviews, it is politically significant that Marty and Rust breach their ideological divide to overcome darkness together.

In the real war going on "underneath things" in which values of the Republic are threatened by the private interest of Empire, light just might have a shot against darkness if we are able to trust intuition over appearance and accept both the power and the limits of individualism. But that would take watching our national tragedy unfold on TV as if we had something real at stake.

Sun Ra, Live in Central Park

Sun Ra

SummerStage was established by the Central Park Conservancy to bring a diverse selection of music to the park in a series of free performances during the summer months. The first concert was held at the Naumberg Bandshell in 1986 and featured the Sun Ra Arkestra.

In 1986, our gang didn't venture uptown much—anything north of 14th Street (or west of Broadway, for that matter)—was considered terra non grata. We didn't like sunshine or the outdoors so much either. But a Sun Ra show? Free? OK, all aboard the 6 train (or, the A Train maybe?)! As long as we could get back downtown by nightfall.

I remember 1986 as a particularly unpleasant year, for the most part. I was heartbroken, lonely and depressed and was working shitty temp jobs on Wall Street and drinking too much. But I remember this day very well, 'cause the show put a big smile on my face. I was very happy to have the chance to hear it again. Get your ticket here!

—*B. Kold*

Personnel (best guess):
Sun Ra—*piano, synthesizer, vocals*
Randall Murray—*trumpet*
Tyrone Hill—*trombone*
Pat Patrick—*alto saxophone, clarinet*
Marshall Allen—*alto saxophone, flute, piccolo, oboe*
Danny Ray Thompson—*alto saxophone, baritone saxophone, flute, bongos*
John Gilmore—*tenor saxophone, clarinet, timbales*
Eloe Omoe—*alto saxophone, alto clarinet, bass clarinet*
James Jacson—*bassoon, Ancient Egyptian Infinity Drum*
Ronald Wilson—*tenor saxophone*
Carl LeBlanc—*electric guitar*
Tyler Mitchell—*bass*
Thomas Hunter, Earl "Buster" Smith—*drums*

1. Intro
2. Improv #1 (featuring guest Billy Bang)
3. Stardust from Tomorrow
4. Improv #2
5. Improv #3
6. Prelude to a Kiss
7. Take the A Train (part 1)
8. Take the A Train (part 2)
9. East of the Sun
10. Slumming on Park Avenue
11. Swing Instrumental
12. I Dream Too Much
13. Space Is the Place--> We Travel the Spaceways

Listen: www.sensitiveskinmagazine.com/sun-ra-live-central-park-1986/

The Year of Our Lord Quetzalcoatl

Margarita Shalina

THE MORNING OF THE FIRST DAY IN THE Dark Zone, I wake, still dreaming in black and white. I am Joan Crawford. I am Mildred Pierce. In the black of night, a storm is raging. I am in a bungalow by the ocean. The white foam waves crash on the beach. I dress frantically in the dark and run out the front door.

Significant Other is behind me shouting and grumbling, slowing me down. It's noon. Epic lines are forming at the pizzerias where gas-burning ovens are cooking in the dark. We walk westward along St. Mark's Place between 2nd and 3rd Avenue. I remind myself that, as a post-modern woman, I know how to starve. Throngs of curious people are out looking about. Everyone has a camera. Not cell phones but big proper cameras are hanging around people's necks as they traverse the streets. Sig's eyes are soft and sad, observant, downcast.

"This is the fourth one of these that I've lived through," Sig says.

"Don't get ahead of yourself. The lights aren't back on yet," I reply.

"This is the fourth one of these that I've lived through," Sig says.

"Don't get ahead of yourself. The lights aren't back on yet," I reply.

"My father died in the 1977 blackout. His respirator failed."

"I was four in 1977. You would have been arrested for child molestation." Sig looks over at my face and smiles.

We arrive at St. Mark's Bookshop and it is closed. Owner is nowhere to be found. I stand peering through the front door, rattling the keys in my hand, wondering whether to go in. I decide it's pointless. Some of the Cooper Union Maintenance Crew are in front of the dorm. They call out to us and wave. We return to the apartment on 4th and First.

Our super is standing sentinel at the front door and Sig joins him while I go upstairs to shower quickly in the dark and wash my longish, dirty hair. We have hot water. Super's eyes are also observant but worried. Sig and he do that thing that men do where they cite the obvious to one another and call it an exchange of vital information.

My mother is upstairs knitting in half-light with a candle burning. I dress intentionally. I put on rain boots even though it's not raining anymore and exit the apartment to rejoin Sig who asks what the hell has taken me so long. Sig's twin brother, Ass Grabber, and his wife Stripper Brows, have migrated north from Chinatown in search of supplies. It's impressive that they've found us since no one's cell phone works. Stripper Brows emerges from the bowels of our local deli's darkened corners, with hard salami triumphantly raised over her head in one hand like a Sandinista holding up an AK-47. Her black Brussels Griffin is in the other. A can of tuna is pressed awkwardly to her chest. The focus turns to acquiring alcohol and it's decided that the only liquor store which could be open is in Chinatown by the Manhattan Bridge. We all take a walk down there. I stand half-listening to their decisions and not focusing on their conversation, resenting that I have to be swept up in a crowd when I have concerns of my own. They prattle on about how to plan the first night. They talk about dinner. They always talk about dinner.

I meditate on how to get in contact with Owner. I stand staring into my hand, flexing it open then closing it into a knot, trying to remember life before cell phones. Being teenage in the Village and traveling in packs from park to park, packs of urchins in search of love or drugs. My teenage voice appears in my head in a shadowy memory. *We'll be on the benches in Tompkins Square Park,* it says to someone somewhere in time. Calling my mother on a payphone at 1AM loaded, screaming, *I'm not dead! Please open the door when I knock?* There used to be a way of calling for free by unfurling a paper clip and sticking one end into a hole of the receiver's mouthpiece and the other end into the key slot in the square metal drawer that the quarters are deposited into. The paper clip forms a conduit between these two holes. Something short-circuits and you hear a click. Then you can call the world.

"Ah, shit, I'm a moron," I mutter rhetorically, bolting across the street ignoring disaster-tourism traffic—cars from outside the Dark Zone driving with no traffic lights just for thrills. I'd forgotten about payphones. I dig through my wallet for quarters left over from preemptive hurricane laundry, fish out my planner, look up the number.

"Hello?" A woman's voice comes on the phone.

"Hey! Hi! Owner's Wife?! It's Margarita. Is Owner there? You're on 14th, no? Are you blacked out? I stopped by the shop. Are you OK?" She starts to respond, then Owner comes on the line in mid-sentence.

"Hi, Margarita. We're all right but we're in a high rise. No water or power. It's OK though, because we're just on the second floor so I can come and go." Heroic Owner has arthritis. Heroic Owner's Wife is battling cancer.

"What do you want to do? Are we going to open?"

"No."

"OK. But I'm here. Sig has offered to volunteer for the cause. I texted with TLS Hipster last night, I bet I can find him. Plus we can probably figure a way of getting in contact with SoHo-Anonymous. And there's you and Owner No. 2. That makes six. Are you sure you don't want to open?"

"No. Wait until the power's back on."

* * *

Wednesday morning the sun rises and floods my mother's living room. I wake slowly, nuzzling into Sig's hairy chest and out of habit gently reach for his soft Sphinx cat penis curled in slumber. I throw on leggings and a cotton sweater then stumble into the kitchen to make coffee. We're all a little hung over from screwdrivers, compliments of Sig, and drinks and dinner at Ass Grabber's place the night before. Sig, mother and I are triangulating between the three apartments out of necessity. Yesterday afternoon Sig led me into a liquor store unprompted and picked out the biggest bottle of Stoli he could find. "People! Alcohol! Civilization!" I squealed, clapping my hands as we entered the darkened shop on Grand Street.

I pack a flask and we go out to see the transformer, Sig and I. There are cars marooned at weird angles all along eastern most 14th Street, by Stuyvesant Town. We see a lime-green VW bug with driftwood through its passenger window at a diagonal to the curb.

"Should we all like, be taking Chlorella tablets or something?" I remark, looking at the Con Ed structure struggling back to life.

"What, you mean Fukushima? That was a nuclear power plant. We're fine."

"Yeah? What powers the power station, then? What does that thing run on? What does it eat? Sig, it blew up and we're right on top of it."

East River Park is trashed and blocked off by police cars. We turn south on C. No one in the neighborhood can get cell service and only ground lines work. I keep hearing passers-by in the street saying, "That cheap-ass MetroPCs still works." I turn to Sig and mutter, "I have MetroPCs and my cheap-as-shit ghetto service is *not* working."

There is a pocket of reception on the SW corner of Avenue C and 9th Street. About 30 people are crowded together yelling "I'm all right!" to somebody, somewhere. The crowd grows as more people passing by stop to inquire why we're all standing there, then retrieve their cell phones and smile relieved at being able to make contact with the world outside the Dark Zone.

Eateries take it to the street and serve hot food from aluminum containers warmed by gel fuel canisters. Sig buys himself a taco with rice and beans. He hands me a second fork and I pick from it nervously while we walk. Bars and restaurants are open by candlelight and flames glow and jump about illuminating smiling profiles as we pass. C Squat, a/k/a the Museum of Reclaimed Urban Space on Avenue C, has taken its generator onto the street and is cooking food for the neighborhood, recharging phones. Anarchist punk squatters know how to survive and well, Sig and I comment to one another and beam *old-skool* neighborhood pride at them. We continue along Avenue C and Sig comments on piles of furniture at the curbside with CDs and DVDs stacked on top of a sofa.

"Is that Bowie?"

"Yeah, but it's late Bowie." I reply.

A middle-aged woman in serious rainboots and a gray slicker walking up the block overhears us and starts laughing. "That's my stuff." She resembles a fisherman. Sig apologizes for perusing her belongings and returns the CD.

"You got flooded?" He asks the obvious.

"Yeah," she says, turning toward a below-street-level apartment in a very low-rise tenement the front door of which is wide open. "Water wrecked the place. We had to pump it. All this shit is ruined. Oh, well. It's just stuff, right? You can keep the Bowie."

We continue along Avenue C and notice generators loudly pumping basements of businesses and restaurants, water flowing freely down the block, opposite of the way it came. The sun is setting and the streets are turning a murky grey. Flashlights begin to appear on the streets in loose wrists. Rays of light shine left to right across the pavement. Bright beams of light blind us as we approach. Nocturnal vision kicks into full gear.

East River Park is trashed and blocked off by police cars. We turn south on C. No one in the neighborhood can get cell service and only ground lines work.

"It'll be night soon. What do you want to do about dinner?" Sig asks randomly. "Do you want to go to Brooklyn to buy food? We can walk over the Williamsburg Bridge. Then go back to your mom's place and cook." Sig and I have an electric stove while mother's is gas.

"Yeah, let's do that. Sig, listen, I think we should go to Spoonbill & Sugartown. They're our friends. We'll ask to recharge our phones and maybe they'll even let us use their internet. Maybe we'll even see Chelsea Girl or run into TLS Hipster there. I want *news* really badly right now."

"Me too," he says, kissing me on the forehead and we sway east and further south to the bridge, which at that moment is the most crowded I've ever seen it in my entire life with the possible exceptions of 9/11 and the MTA strikes.

We're in a blackout in lower Manhattan. We walk through an autumnal gloaming. Williamsburg is bright and lovely and alive with power. Their electricity is not being held hostage. The bridge is literally half lit. The lights lining the bridge on the Brooklyn side are on beginning precisely in the middle of its long red torso's expanse four hundred feet above the East River. Light beckons from Brooklyn as night falls fast. We pass from Manhattan into Brooklyn as though we're walking out of a dark cave into the light, a parade of refugees going toward salvation. We turn left onto Bedford Avenue. Something knocks into my leg and I look down.

A tiny ballerina has pirouetted out of control. A woman wearing a black leather jacket, a silver eye-mask and cat whiskers apologizes and pulls the little tulle thing by the hand out of my way. Tiny Firemen, little Supermen, miniscule Batmen come at us as a mob led by adults with cat tails and strollers appear. "Awww, was that a munchkin Silver Surfer?" I ask looking back as Sig pulls me along. A roadkill traffic cop with a mangled face barking directions at a small laughing witch and a spinning unicorn knocking into one another appear as a frontline before us.

All the traffic lights are on. The street is illuminated by shop windows. All of a sudden there is so much light—multicolored neon of blues and yellows and reds and noise and people and the exuberant voices of children, everywhere. A swarm of tiny cheering, discombobulated things hopped up on sugar, somehow simultaneously wandering in circles while being ushered forward by their minders. They hold plastic orange pumpkin head pails out at tiny arm's length to every passing stranger. Bedford has been taken over. It is impenetrable. They spill into the street bringing oncoming traffic to a halt. My head reels. I feel like I'm tripping—all the colors, all the lights, all the noise—but in a bad way and it's all happening way too fast.

"Sig, it's Halloween. I'd forgotten about

#88 No Logo, painting by David de Biasio

Halloween. Lower Manhattan must have thrown up every last tiny costumed beastie to panhandle candy on Bedford." I look up and realize that I'm talking to no one and feel nervous that the breeders might take offense and turn on me. Sig is half a block ahead. I run negotiating the masses and noise to catch up and grab his corduroyed arm, letting him lead while I look back as we continue along Bedford.

Collagist looks up from behind the register when we enter Spoonbill & Sugartown. Her big warm eyes soften and smile a greeting at us. "Hi," Sig and I mutter one after the other, smirking pathetically, a little embarrassed for some reason.

The store is packed.

"Collagist, would it be awful if we recharged our phones?"

"Oh, of course not," she says reassuringly, gesturing for us to come behind the counter where Sig is already sniffing around for an outlet.

"Would it be too much to ask if I could possibly get online, too? Actually and, more importantly, have you seen TLS Hipster?" My speech is a nervous staccato. She laughs softly. "He's here, in back. Go ahead. Just behind the curtain. Go on." She draws back the curtain to reveal TLS Hipster slouching face-first into the Mac's large flatscreen. He turns his head after a minute, then rises and approaches, says my name and we hug like survivors reunited in a refugee camp.

"What's the good word?" I ask, gesturing toward the Mac.

"There are all these terrible fires in parts of the Rockaways. Breezy Point burned down. Coney Island got hit hard too. All the high rises are blacked out," Hip responds.

"Isn't Breezy Point that weird community with all the awful zoning and parking regulations that pretend they're a gated community with a private beach but really aren't?"

"Yes," Hip responds.

"Those people are assholes," I mutter.

"Still, no one deserves that," Hip gently admonishes me.

"You're right. I'm sorry." I say, lowering my head and nodding. "We have to call Owner, TLS. Have you been in contact?"

"Yeah, I've called him every day so far. I have a ground line."

"Right. Right! I've spoken to him, too. I want to open, Hip." His simultaneous response of "—Open! Let's call him. We'll call in the mall." His focus shifts abruptly. We're standing behind the counter of Spoonbill as a young man approaches to make a purchase. He is accompanied by a nondescript but attractive male cohort and a beautiful disaffected skinny woman with pin-straight blonde hair. "Margarita! This is Xeno's friend Siberia! I must! Introduce you," TLS Hipster says emphatically. "Hello, it's so nice to meet you. I'm Siberia," the beautiful young man says in Russian while reaching over the counter and extending his hand. He looks exceptionally Russo-Asiatic. Fashionably dressed in tight dark blue jeans and a black leather jacket that hits the waist, with a knit black cap over jet-black silky hair and thin slits revealing ice blue eyes, his skin all rosewater, his features all pointing east. "Huh?" I ask, distracted. "Yes, hello. I'm Margarita." I respond too formally, weakly shaking his hand while moving away from the counter.

"And there's Xeno! You've never really met," Hip says, leading me between the bookcases. Xeno is an adorable nerd boy synth player who tours prolifically and internationally. He was a Russophile before he discovered Hungary. "Xeno is learning Russian!" Hip exclaims. "No, I'm not touring Russia! I'm going to Hungary," Xeno yells over the noise of the teeming crowd and loud synth music. We can all mostly hear one another but are losing track of the conversation. "Hungarian is one of the weirdo languages. If you speak Russ, that won't make sense for learning Hungarian, Estonia or Finnish," I mutter absentmindedly but loudly, making myself semi-heard while scanning the room, plotting a course to the street. "Yeah, I know that. That's why I'm learning Hungarian!" Xeno shouts. I'm making my exit with my eye on the front door as he makes an attempt at noble conversation in Russian: "Yes, Margarita. I've heard much about you from TLS Hipster. I'm getting ready to tour Europe. What do you think about . . . " He's at my side and I turn to face him.

"Xeno," I say in plain English. "I've wanted to meet you for a long time, too. I really dig your music, truly, but I have to apologize. I need to . . . just get some water. I'm just going to the store. I don't mean to be rude. I'm a little over-stimulated right now. And I really want water. I apologize." He looks at me oddly and backs off as I run toward the front door traversing beautiful Brooklyn's prosperous American refugees who've fled the heart of the country for the heart of the world. They've packed the store. They browse in unison.

I bolt through the front door into Halloween child madness and blessed fresh air, navigating through them. They are oblivious, staring up into the night's light and yelling nonsensically at parents and friends. I walk past stores until I find one that makes sense, enter and buy a bottle of lime seltzer, cracking the seal to drink while standing on line. Children barge in between each exchange, screaming – "TRICK OR TREAT!!! TRICK OR TREAT!!!" I walk back slow, taking my time, sipping seltzer and wondering when begging candy off of grocery stores became acceptable.

When I return, Hipster touches my arm gently and we retreat through the second entrance of Spoonbill into the mall area, where tiny panhandling children knock into us as 20-something gazelles in full make-up shout audibly about their hook-ups and booty calls and party plans for the night in voices and personalities indistinguishable from one another.

"*You* look beautiful!"

"No! You! Look beautiful…!"

"Text hime already!!!"

I turn my head back to Hip as he dials Heroic Owner's number while my own cell phone is left unattended recharging somewhere behind the counter of the bookstore. We exchange looks in dim amber light by the entrance to the mall and entreat them to open the shop to no avail. Hip points out to Owner that Spoonbill is doing amazing business while we're bleeding money. We encourage Owner to at the very least take his wife, leave their apartment and cab it to Brooklyn or Midtown for a hot meal in a restaurant, but they have that distinctly provincial quality that older Manhattanites who've lived in the same neighborhood for decades acquire. Brooklyn may as well be Beijing and north of 14th Street Helsinki. Hip clips his mobile shut and we return to Spoonbill stopping at their wall of art books.

Spectacle Theatre enters with his remarkable hair. Sig and Xeno walk over to join us. "Awww, look who's here," Hip announces and we all greet TLS Hipster's thin ex-girlfriend, Butterscotch Lick, as she approaches smiling in all her cerebral adorableness. We begin catching up on one another's ordeals. The Brooklynites interrogating the Manhattanites admit sheepishly that all is well and normal, even dull, in their neck of the woods.

TLS Hipster turns to Sig and me: "Are you two walking back to Manhattan now?"

"Yeah, as soon as our phones are charged, we're going to get food, then walk back over the bridge before it gets too late," Sig replies.

"Stick to the main roads, and all that. You can gentrify the shit out of it all you want but it's still the LES in a blackout and tonight's Halloween," I add.

"Man! It's like the fucking Warriors!" Spectacle exclaims and I can't help but hold up two fingers and the thumb of one hand and tap them together menacingly—"Clink! Clink! Clink! Clink! Warr-i-ors. Come out to pla-y-ay. Warr-i-ors! Come out to pla-y-ay! WARR-I-ORS!" Suddenly we're all screeching it in unison until the word devolves into laughter.

"I have no idea what any of you are doing." A confused, wide-eyed Butterscotch Lick says, surveying us as though we've all gone mad.

"Awww, man!" Spectacle begins, "You've never seen *The Warriors?* It's a movie. A classic! They're in this gang, right?"

"Their gang is called the Warriors," TLS adds, smiling softly at her.

"They're from Coney Island but they go all the way up to the Bronx to some like, UN peace, gang accord, rally thingy," I continue.

"Nooo! Not peace, Cyrus is trying to unify the gangs to take over New York," TLS says, correcting him.

"It takes place in 1979, when New York almost went bankrupt," Sig offers.

"But Cyrus is shot during his big speech and the

Warriors are framed for his murder. *Escape from New York* is another amazing movie from that era," Spectacle continues.

"So they have to get home, all the way from the Bronx down to Coney Island, through three boroughs and, in the process, they have to go through every single other gang's territory. And everybody is after them because there's a call out to avenge Cyrus's murder. They have to fight their way through. But all the other gangs are really silly," I add.

"Like the Furies," TLS says, laughing in spite of himself as Butterscotch furrows her brow and takes it all in very seriously nodding as though at a grad level critical theory lecture.

"Which are the Furies?" Sig asks.

"Oh, they're on roller-skates with Kiss face paint and baseball bats wearing those Babe Ruth uniforms," TLS explains.

"The Warriors are led by this really good-looking tortured shirtless blonde dude wearing a leather vest named Swan," I add.

"They're all shirtless. They're all wearing leather vests," Sig says rolling his eyes.

"Swan—How hot is that?!" I smile suggestively and nod at Butterscotch.

"That's Michael Beck. Walter Hill directed it." Sig adds.

"Michael Beck was also in the classic, *Xanadu*," TLS says sarcastically.

"I LOVE *XANADU!*" I squeal as everyone bursts out laughing and Butterscotch gets even more confused. "It's about the seven muses, you know, from Greek mythology and one of them, played by Olivia Newton John, falls in love with Swan in a roller rink, but Zeus, her father, totally does not approve. It's a musical. *Xan-a-duuuu*," I start singing.

"Isn't *The Warriors* based on a novel?" Sig asks.

"Sol Yurick!" TLS directs the response back at him.

"Maybe I should screen *The Warriors*," Spectacle Theatre says thoughtfully.

"Oh! With *Xanadu!* A Swan double feature," I chime in.

"Alright, it's time for us to go. This one's getting a little . . ." Sig says, leading me away by the arm.

We say our goodbyes and Sig, TLS and I walk up Bedford toward the bridge foraging for food at various stores along the way to the Williamsburg Bridge. Butterscotch accompanies us midway and leaves us at the point on the Bridge where the Dark Zone begins on the Manhattan side. A man and a woman dressed as Magi fall into step with us while walking their bicycles across. My ever untrusting Sig eyes them suspiciously as they try to make conversation.

"Are you supposed to be Magi or two wise men?" I ask. "Yeah, something like that," the male Magi answers. Only assholes say—*something like that*—and anyway, it was a trick question, I think silently to myself as I hug Butterscotch Lick goodbye at the line of demarcation.

"Stick to the main roads, and all that. You can gentrify the shit out of it all you want but it's still the LES in a blackout and tonight's Halloween," I add.

We exit the bridge onto Delancey Street and are met by large NYPD lights powered by portable generators illuminating the roadway of the vehicular exit/entrance to the bridge. "Why is anyone driving?" I anunciate with annoyance.

"Disaster tourism," Sig replies.

"I'll bet none of those people are brain surgeons on call or lawyers with clients on death row. We don't even have the fucking death penalty here! They have no reason to be out. It's dangerous. Especially for us, since we live here," I muttered, growing irritated.

"Who really knows what's going on down here," Sig responds.

"Why are those lights on, for instance?" Hip asks, pointing south as we walk along Delancey.

"That's Seward Park High School. It's been

designated an emergency shelter. There are a lot of disabled, elderly and infirm people out here in the NYCHA projects. I bet someone's on a respirator," I say, looking over at Sig.

"And that other building over there?" Hip asks, pointing at the only other tall structure that has its lights on.

"Don't know," Sig responds.

"It's Gouverneur Hospital. It's really just a glorified high-rise clinic, but they probably have a backup generator. It might be the only thing we have close to a hospital down here, but I don't think they even have an emergency room. St. Vincent's is closed now, so that leaves Beth Israel on 14th, and Bellevue. Is NY Downtown in the Financial District still open?" They both shake their heads contemplatively. "Hey! Do I know my neighborhood, or do I?" I ask, smiling proudly in an attempt to antagonize the boys and keep spirits high as we walk further and further into darkness.

"This is where I leave you," Hip says, turning to face north on Essex. I hug TLS Hipster goodbye as Sig waves.

"Stick to large streets," I shout after him as he disappears into the night. I can't see Houston and Essex from Delancey as he walks away from us and the silhouette of his form merges with the blackness.

Sig and I turn south on Essex and proceed back to my mother's apartment with the spoils of our foraging. We traverse the blackened hallway and enter the apartment where my mother is nervously knitting by candlelight. *Well, she didn't burn the place down*, I think, silently reassured.

Sig proceeds to light candles, making the small apartment come alive and cozy as I mix screwdrivers and prepare a meal of cannelloni beans and quinoa with turmeric. It's Spartan but quick, filling and hot. Everyone's now slightly tipsy, says 'yum' and praises the little meal, but I suspect it's just emotional and physical exhaustion, and the dark heightening our senses, that makes us more appreciative. The dark is making us devolve, or perhaps evolve, depending on how you look at it.

We finish eating and I clear the plates while making more screwdrivers. Sig had laughed at me for buying a whole container of orange juice in Brooklyn and lugging it home over the bridge. He'd made a comment about my having all the wrong priorities, but we're happy to have it now. "Well, you bought us that big pretty jug of Stoli!" I shout toward the living room from the kitchen, laughing at him as he enjoys his blackout cocktail. "What did you expect me to do with it? Is good, no?!" I mock him in an ambiguous Pan-Caucasus semi-Russian accent.

"Horrorshow." Sig replies, nodding drunkenly and making an attempt at remembering the word for *good* in Russian using phonetic transference.

Sig entertains us by making up a trivia quiz, but it doesn't last long since he alone knows all the answers to his own questions. Mom and I accuse him of cheating. The game falls apart when I return to the living room, having scraped the dishes clean in the kitchen, putting the trash into sealed plastic bags and tying them. My mother retreats to bed.

I look out the window at the buildings across from us and see beams from flashlights and the dancing flames of candles in some of the other windows. He approaches and stands behind me, cupping his hands around my upper arms, reassuringly.

"We have the best lit place in the apocalypse," I say softly, looking up at Sig behind me. We are surrounded by silence and stillness.

He removes his clothes unprompted, dropping them on the armchair to the right of the window flanked by paintings and climbs into bed on the pullout couch. I touch the plants to the left of the windowsill, watching my neighbors' lights flicker, then I walk through the apartment to make sure every last candle has been extinguished. I undress in the dark, placing my clothes adjacent to his and climb onto the pullout couch, curling fetal under the blankets. I close my eyes and make my internal darkness one with the darkness that surrounds us.

an excerpt from The Year of Our Lord Quetzalcoatl

Photographs

Dennis Gordon

I've been drawn to abandoned buildings all my life. When I was a boy, the allure was breaking into forbidden places without getting caught, the adventure of making new discoveries. Later, when I became a firefighter in 1978 in the South Bronx, entering and navigating vacant structures became both a full time job and a passion. Around the same time, I moved to the Lower East Side, where I was surrounded by blocks of vacant tenements dating back to the early 1900s. Despite how dangerous this was, I spent much of my time inside exploring. Over the years my attraction to abandoned spaces grew and I fell in love with turn-of-the-century industries: mills, warehouses, foundries, loft buildings and factories. This includes former institutions, such as asylums, prisons, schools and hospitals. And also foreclosed homes.

Photographing these emptied spaces, I began to feel comfortable in the midst of the neglect and decay. The abandonment, loneliness and isolation inside the structures grounded me. I discovered an escape from the boredom of inhabited spaces, growing lost within the wealth of bygone architecture and design. Here, I feel like I'm participating in some grand installation of living art. The decay is dynamic and the interiors will be different when I revisit them in a year.

New levels of rust and mold. Brick disintegrating and nature slowly prevailing, replacing manmade elements. Where some people see eyesores, I see the labor of architects, craftsmen and assemblymen who used complex machines built as durably as the products they made. To me, each abandoned building tells a story about our past, and all these buildings tell a collective story of our present, an era of greed when everything—from architecture to wares to art—is disposable, replaceable.

My artwork recreates and memorializes the emotional experience of seeing and exploring these structures. I also want to pay tribute to the quality of manufacturing we once had and the domestic jobs it created.

—Dennis Gordon

CAT
HER
INE
KILL
PK

RUSK

Lambs to the Laughter

Anonymous

I HAVE THE KIND OF MIND THAT WOULD KILL me if it didn't need me for transportation.

In this case to Ireland.

I had no conscious desire to go anywhere near the place but somehow I found myself sucked into the subway, placed on a plane and bundled onto a bus for Kilkenny. Before I was even fully awake, I was faced with the house I grew up in and a sky cracked with crows. Would I be welcome? Had I any right to be there? Why was I so nervous? Who was that in the upstairs window? I was thrilled to see it was my oldest brother Brian. It meant that I wouldn't have to sound the alarm-like doorbell and wake the rest of them up.

Anticipating his sarcastic signature handshake, in which a folded index finger wiggled against the interior of my palm, I selected my wryest smile. But it was wasted, since his hand merely gestured where I'd be staying. I'd be sleeping on a little fold-up camper-bed nudged against a radiator that, as far as I could remember, had never felt heat. This was because the *good room* was reserved for visiting priests and was therefore rarely used. Placement here defined you as an outsider.

I normally slept upstairs, but since Connor, my other brother, had moved back a few months previously, my old room was now his. Vapor leapt in and out of Brian's throat. As a dedicated member of datemedotcom, I was relieved to hear that thanks to his online poker habit, there was now quite a decent Internet connection in the house. I had already sent countless cut-and-paste emails to childless women under 34, no taller than 5'8", with bodies described as *thin,* presenting my trip home as a sort of voluntary international one-man rescue mission. I looked forward to checking my inbox for the gush of approval that would surely follow.

I unpacked my "Williamsburg bestseller" debut novel and my "cure for second-book-syndrome" and arranged them carefully on a chair by the camper-bed. They would ward off evil. Almost immediately a shadow fell over them and a figure filled the doorway as the *good room* got one degree colder. Was I expected to believe this was Connor? He was so very changed and old-looking. Squeezing the hardened hand he offered me, I felt his index finger tickle my palm.

"She's too much, I'm going to have to move back to New York."

I had no idea how to react, since the handshake seemed to ironize the information. It didn't help that we'd hardly spoken in ten years. A phone call at Christmas, if that.

"Welcome home," he said, "such as it is," and released my hand at last. Unable to think of anything to say, I nodded far too cheerfully.

"We'll need forty Euros for the kitty at some point, but don't worry about it now."

He was referring to the communal fund for groceries he'd put himself in charge of.

"Why? Do we have a cat now?" I said and immediately regretted it.

"I hope you come up with better lines than that in your books," he said, nodding at my little library. I produced the rashers and eggs I'd bought for breakfast.

"Oh that'll go down well. We'll deduct it from your weekly amount. You don't have the receipt do you?"

I confessed that I did not. He nodded professionally, as if making a mental note of a new employee. One to watch out for. It wasn't official yet because he was still waiting for a means test and an interview but there was a very good chance that Connor would get paid a salary to pretend he gave a shit about his mother. It was a phenomenon reverently referred to in social service circles as A Carer's Allowance.

"So you're a writer now."

The sarcasm was conspicuously absent.

"I suppose so yeah."

"I went to a play the other night and I definitely got the bug. So you might find I'll be getting into the writing game meself. . . . Ahh, yes, the *thee-at-tur*."

It was irritating to hear him go on about how he'd already been writing for years, as if I were the one copying him. He had always been viciously competitive and, even now, looking depleted enough to be one of mother's contemporaries, he could siphon up my insecurities. What if he managed to write something decent? How mortifying for me. Could he actually do it? He also talked about doing stand-up. This was something he might actually be able to pull off. The Annual Kilkenny Comedy Festival would provide the perfect platform for his talents—talents that were still very much in evidence. Over a breakfast of rashers and eggs, Brian, the least talented storyteller in our family, took it upon himself to relate how one night a *fucking hipster* made the mistake of bragging to them in the local pub.

"I co-own an arts collective," he says. And guess what Connor said?"

I shook my head.

"We co-couldn't give a fuck."

Connor held my gaze as Brian enthused but there was no pleasure in it for him. I felt deep shame over my kitty comment and sympathy for the hipster. I knew what it was like to be broadsided by Connor. The familiar feeling of humiliation warmed me up.

I was home.

At least he wasn't talking about converting the house into a bed and breakfast.

He had always talked about how the Yanks would pay a fortune to stay in an Irish house. Lose this wall, it wasn't load-bearing anyway, and re-hang those doors to face the front, bung in a few extra beds and you'd be all set. There was no mention of how he drank his own house from under himself in the Bronx.

If I could just get through the following few weeks I'd be back in New York where I hoped to get a play of my own happening. A Broadway producer had asked me to adapt *Diary of an Oxygen Thief* for the stage. It was where my attention belonged. All I had to do was soak up some authentic Irish heritage and nod convincingly left and right for a few weeks and there'd be no need to show my face for another six years.

Maybe even longer.

Meanwhile Brian's email describing mother as *frail and bitchy* proved accurate.

It was irritating to hear him go on about how he'd already been writing for years, as if I was the one copying him. . . . What if he managed to write something decent? How mortifying for me.

"Oh, there he is. Is he still bald?"

"Yes ma he is." I started to remove my woolen hat.

"Oh Jesus leave it on I don't want to see it. Who bought the rashers?"

She had deflated since I'd seen her last. Her knuckles were new to me.

"Turn on the television. It might warm up the room."

Every program talked about the economy or the lack of it and how to conserve energy or the lack of it and who was bankrupt and how generally fucked we all were and how maybe we deserved it for being so fucking cocky in the first place. Even Gay Byrne had been jolted out of retirement to do interviews with fellow fuck-ups who lost all their money to bad investments. Drunk driving was no longer tolerated (one pint and you lost your license) and smoking was actually *banned* from pubs. Lavish banquets in legendary venues went unattended, since punters preferred to hold parties at home. Strange days indeed when an Irish pub went unsuckled. It made me wonder how Connor could still afford to drink. And smoke.

painting by Julie Torres

The answer was right in front of me. I pretended to be preoccupied with my phone as he supervised the signing over of our mother's pension to him. Had he waited for me to be present to do this? Was I in fact a witness? Her signature authorized him to withdraw a weekly cash-payment from the post office. She was getting too old to pick it up herself and this supposedly saved her the trip. He was also newly empowered to pick up her weekly doctor's prescription from the chemist. Representing in excess of four hundred Euros a week and an endless supply of free drugs, I'd have thought he'd be a little more civil, but her refusal to wear a hearing aid was an invitation, not just to shout at her but at all of us. Opening the door to the hallway, Brian gestured to me to follow. The shouting continued from the kitchen as he lowered his voice to a whisper.

"It was worse when first came home, he came home rat-arsed one night looking for his cab fare after losing seven hundred Euros playing poker. *"You brought two addictions home with you,"* I said. *"Drinking and gambling; either you stop or you can fuck off back to the States."*

He let this sink in.

"He's been a bit better since."

I shivered at the thought of Connor leeching off a life that even our mother didn't want. She longed to be with her late husband. To her, the very act of eating postponed their reunion.

"He's hoping to hold out until his allowance comes through," I said. "In the meantime he'll get by on her prescriptions.

It was my turn to let it sink in.

"I see this all the time in AA. Someone's mother gets cancer and the son drops everything to come home and help out with the free supply of morphine patches."

Brian looked as if the idea was ridiculous. But not impossible.

"You think he's that bad?"

I had plenty more to say but decided instead to get myself to a meeting. The town's depressing atmosphere was refreshed almost hourly by what appeared to be grey paint drizzling from the sky. At every turn I was confronted with stunningly beautiful girls smiling from inside carefully lit posters. Girls so far removed from the reality of what wobbled past me on the streets of Kilkenny, someone should have been prosecuted for fraud.

When I got back, I was told that mother had fallen and hit her head on the downstairs bathroom sink. Brian bandaged her with what he could find: kitchen-towels and sellotape. I didn't ask where Connor was.

My sister Grainne was due for a quick visit but she never stayed in the house. Over the years she'd learned to make other arrangements, partly because there was no room and partly because the house was so cold but mostly because her husband was so unwelcome. She stayed across the road at the Shannondale Hotel. Rates were even lower than normal now since the country was more bankrupt than usual. I fantasized about using the shower over there. No way I was ever taking my jacket off in that house so the idea of stepping naked into a shower was laughable. Even in my creaky little bed I wore my woolen hat and socks. I couldn't think of worse conditions for an eighty-six-year-old woman; a freezing house with two life-sized parasites feeding off her.

Three, if you counted me.

But within a half-hour of Grainne's arrival, mother soiled herself on the threshold of the upstairs bathroom. The smell was strangely sweet and disgusting at the same time. She had almost made it. Ordinarily she used the downstairs toilet but perhaps wanting to impress her well-to-do daughter she had embarked on the ardous expedition upstairs.

I had to admit I was glad to have been at another meeting at the time (I was going to one every day now) and Brian had to be happy to be at work. The Carer was not available for comment, which meant Grainne wasn't home an hour before she had tears in her eyes and shit on her hands. She had lost her unpopular husband to cancer the year before and was somehow expected to take this in her stride because *Grainne was a trooper* and *nothing gets Grainne down.*

It should have been unbearably sad but I had become hardened. My own tribulations of heartbreak and penury in New York had inspired all manner of fortification to the point that I was now pretty much unbreachable. My priority was to inflect Grainne's understanding in the same way I had done with Brian.

"An alcoholic will steal your money and help you look for it," I said.

"You should know," she said quickly.

Connor and Grainne had always been close.

Every evening after dinner Connor and Brian flanked their mother with identical laptops and headphones playing online poker while she watched mostly news on TV. I edited them both out of my carefully crafted cut-and-paste messages that portrayed me as the heroically returned son who could be relied on by his poor ailing mother for at least the rest of the month. The fireplace was worried over like a sick child and gave out about as much heat.

But all I got was one hesitant response from a shapely looking tutor of French literature and film. I was far from procuring the sexual attention I had hoped since my brutally honest, tell-all fictionalised memoir had become a liability. She had no desire, she said, to become the "latest conquest in a darkly hilarious cult classic." Fair enough, but what was the point of writing a book if it didn't get you laid?

I began to master the art of sleeping.

The solution was simple. When the various inmates tottered off to their cells, you sleep in the common room. Brian frowned when I brought up the idea of sharing Grainne's hotel room for a few nights.

"Don't put her in that position."

Pretty rich coming from a guy living off his mother but I was happy to hear the firmness in his voice since it meant that he might stand up to Connor when the time came. As the eldest brother, he was the natural father figure and I was secretly happy that he seemed OK with this. I was a child all over again testing out the barriers of what I could and could not get away with and it was a relief to reach the limits of my rebellion. He did however approve of my using the shower. The very idea. A hot shower in a warm bathroom with fluffy white towels and . . .

"Don't forget you still owe me forty Euros." Connor's voice was urgent behind me.

It might have been jetlag or sleeplessness or frustration at being harassed for a debatable debt, but my mouth opened and out it jumped.

"Go fuck . . ."

He had smoked me out. The real me, the one he knew I was hiding. The old me. The real me. His suspicions were confirmed. All my AA bullshit was just an act. And he had yet to hold me up to ridicule for being arrogant enough to announce myself as a writer. The laughable idea that the thoughts and ideas slithering around in my wet brain were worthy of preservation. I steeled myself. Surely this was his chance. But no tirade came.

Instead I was allowed to marinate in my own juices.

Was it a ploy? He was preparing the ground for his own writing career. Any success I had would pave the way for his own. The moment I heard he'd moved back home I wanted to cancel my trip but it would have been too obvious and anyway I had already booked it. Ever since I quit drinking we were deeply uncomfortable in each other's presence. And there he stood not quite looking at me but allowing me to look at him. The better to register his disappointment.

I needed a wash.

Brian got up at 7AM every morning and drank a cup of tea in the gloom. Having denied himself electric light and the warmth of a gas heater he was only just worthy of the power it took to boil the kettle. I had just finished stowing away my camper bed when a letter shoved itself surreally through the letter-box. Immediately apparent were the three blue castles of the Kilkenny County Council logo. I placed it on the kitchen table where Brian would see it when he turned around.

"Do you want to bring it up to him?"

It was a sly suggestion that might help diffuse the built-up tension between his younger brothers but I only agreed because there was a good chance it contained a rejection. The exhaled stink of alcohol and tobacco was thick in the air as I approached the hump of blankets on top of what used to be my bed. I waited for him to wake up and curse me but instead he was uncharacteristically polite as he fingered the letter open. I stood there like a royal messenger looking directly ahead and there on the wall was a picture of myself at twelve years old making my Holy Communion. The word *freak* was written in biro across my forehead.

He was approved to proceed to the next stage of his application. Means-test and interview date to follow. Within seconds he began to worry that my presence in the house would affect his chances.

"You're not mentioned anywhere in the application, it could get tricky if . . ."

If what? Was I supposed to agree that I was in the way? Would I have to pretend to be a fucking lodger? A tenant from the States. I'd lost weight since I stopped drinking and as a result I now looked more like my brothers than ever before. For years there had been a standing joke that because I was so unlike my siblings I had to have been fathered by the milkman. Mother would shriek with delighted laughter at this, especially since the milkman was no oil painting. She could be an evil little fucker when she wanted to be. A few weeks before I arrived home while waiting for Connor to have his neck looked at by her doctor (on her insurance) she had grown impatient.

"What's he doing in there?" she asked the receptionist. "Fucking him?"

Connor told this story as evidence of the hardships he'd had to endure and yes he might have made it up but she was capable of it.

I consoled myself that there had to be a great Irish play in all of this.

It had all the prerequisites of misery, penury, rivalry and alcoholism.

Granted, someone might need to starve to death or drown in a river but with three weeks left there was every reason to be optimistic.

As the narrator of the play I'd make it clear that though I portrayed my brothers as living off my mother I too was guilty of mining the situation for all the Hibernian hubris I could scrape onto a page. In this way the very subject of the play would become evidence of an Irish mother's innate ability to provide for her sons.

Something to ponder on the way to another meeting.

Later that evening Grainne dragged her mother across the road for a free dinner at the Shannondale Hotel. This left all three brothers to dine together for the first time without maternal supervision. A terrible silence descended over the dinner table. We were like strangers forced to sit together in a very bad restaurant. Brian was the first to break the silence.

"Hmmm."

He could have been agreeing with something one of us had said but we hadn't.

No one could say he hadn't kept up *his* end of the conversation. I felt Connor's eyes on me like guns. He was not what you'd call a good cook but he was extremely sensitive so it was necessary to take great care which expression you wore while eating.

"Hmmm," said Brian again or maybe this time it was "Mmmm."

I volunteered to wash the dishes because I knew this was something that would receive universal approval. It inspired another "Hmmm" from Brian, but the carer was less enthusiastic.

"You'll still have to pay your share of the kitty though."

I diverted my rage onto the plates and pots.

The next morning, as I waited for Debbie Barrington to drive in from Thomastown to meet me for breakfast, I studied my face in the window of the High Street Café. Only a week home and I already looked like a rasher-faced culchie. I felt better when she entered though. Her face looked even more ruddy and spud-stuffed than mine.

Her body was a different matter.

It was the product of a different culture. A potato-free democracy that the engnomed inhabitants of Ireland only saw on telly. Its hostess was a youngish history professor who, ignoring the sexual etiquette of the rooms, began chatting to me after an East Village AA meeting. Being newly sober she voiced concerns about an upcoming trip to Ireland to research a book on Oliver Cromwell. Because I knew she'd need staying sober in a country whose national emblem was indistinguishable from a Guinness logo we exchanged details. More to the point I wanted to do to that body what Cromwell did to Ireland.

It wasn't about me, or him or the kitty any more. It was about his active disease of alcoholism versus my active solution for it. I represented the fellowship of Alcoholics Anonymous here. I was a diplomat.

After a comparatively pagan breakfast relying on the combined sacrifices of an average Irish farmyard (everything but the farmer) we toyed with the idea of making Cromwell a more sympathetic character. Maybe he was just an over-enthusiastic philanthropist. Could he have been ahead of his time? An early proponent of euthanasia, perhaps? A precursor to Doctor Kevorkian. A misunderstood enabler of voluntary and or assisted suicide. Surely the fact that he was associated with so many dead only proved how sought after his services were. It was common knowledge that sixteenth-century medical care was non-existent and so the majority of his patients would already have been suffering from all manner of terminal illnesses. It might well transpire that the much-maligned General, far from being the cause of woe, had instead facilitated an *end* to much suffering. In light of these findings Professor Deborah and I might feel duty-bound to petition for his canonization.

"*Blessed Oliver Cromwell* would certainly be a provocative title."

"You got me out of bed today," she said, still laughing.

"Which is ironic," I mewed, "because my intention was to do the opposite."

She bought two signed copies of my books and paid for breakfast.

Connor needed to keep mother alive in the same way a kidnapper needed to keep a hostage healthy. Brian needed to keep a close eye on Connor in case he drank the house out from under all three of them. Mother welcomed the presence of both sons, especially since the alternative was a nursing home.

Son number three suckled on the narrative possibilities.

Maybe Connor's play would interrupt mine in mid-performance. Choreographed to perfection, there would be a sudden but elegant exchange of characters. The actor playing me would now be uglier and considerably fatter, while Connor's new ambassador would be noticeably more muscular, not so much old now as wise. He'd start getting all the good lines while I spent more time downstage only feebly lit by an iPhone. Brian's role would no longer be that of paternal compass but of a weak-willed and easily-led man-child. The hearts and minds of the audience would be drawn to center stage, where Connor's soothing voice helped us navigate the quagmire we had created around him. Brian's failed marriage. Me and my alcoholic self-obsession. Thank God for an embattled hero who sacrifices the freedom and independence of New York so that his mother might enjoy some peace in her final days on this troubled earth.

Or maybe I wouldn't even get a mention, like on the application form.

He didn't appear in my so-called tell-it-all fictionalised memoir, so why should I expect to be featured in his hilariously charming, heartrendingly honest play?

But one character would be consistent in both productions.

The old woman melting into her chair.

Back in the real world, Connor, angry at the very air around him, bellowed left and right while mashing potatoes like the heads of enemies. Apparently he had not been looking forward to my coming home. According to mother he was jealous of me. Even more so, now that I resembled a younger version of him. It occurred to me that whenever I had played down my successes it had always been at her insistence, not his. Was she pitting us against each other? This had been going on for years. It was true he got all the love. What there was of it.

Brian signed up for a speed-dating event but instead of meeting a girl he came home with a friend called Kevin. He announced that he and "Kev" planned to order Chinese that Friday night so there would be one less person to cook for. Connor, grateful for the advance notice, could now more effectively manage expectations of the event.

"Faggots."

I caressed my return ticket. If I could just get through the following nine days I wouldn't have to worry about any of this. I was just a visitor. All I had to do was breathe from the stomach. In. Out. In. Out.

But then he asked for money again.

At first I was calm. I replied reasonably that I'd rather pay my own way and remain separate from the *kitty*. Not very practical, of course, but I hated the idea of being under his command. It wasn't about me, or him or the kitty any more. It was about his active disease of alcoholism versus my active solution for it. I represented the fellowship of Alcoholics Anonymous here. I was a diplomat. I had to show him he couldn't get away with manipulating me or my mother or the situation.

"Fuck you . . . and your fucking kitty."

He stood back, the better to regard me.

"You expect to stay here for free? Is that it? Fine, I'll pay for your food. Would that be OK with you?"

This was delivered, for maximum effect, with mother still in the room but because I was still smiling he took a different tack.

"You're so cheap, so fucking chee—"

"Where's Connor?"

His face quivered.

"What have you done with him? I mean who the fuck are *you?*"

He nodded sadly to himself.

"OK, I see . . . you know what? I don't need this shit either. You can do it . . . see how you fucking like it. I'll go up to Grainne for the week, get the fuck out of this madhouse."

"Fine . . . fuck off up to Grainne, at least we'll have some peace."

"Fine. You can do the cooking, see how thankless a job it is."

Mother spoke suddenly.

"She doesn't want you either."

There was no time to react to this because the gas heater started to sputter.

"Now . . . see? That's more money."

The unbearable pressures of professional carer were back in his face.

"That's another thirty Euros for a new bottle but you don't have to worry, you're outside the kitty, we'll pay for your heating, too, don't worry."

Now that I was effectively excluded from not just the kitty but the family itself he felt comfortable enough to ignore me.

"Ma, do you have thirty Euros for a bottle of gas?"

Vibrating inside her cardigan, she prepared for the epic inconvenience of standing up.

"You can just tell me where it is, I'll get it for you."

His voice was pleading. I couldn't tell if it was a son's frustration at the sight of his immobilized mother or an addict's panic at the notion of money he couldn't get to.

"No," she said too emphatically. "I'll get it meself."

"A houseful of fucking lunatics," he said, genuinely perplexed.

Up until now he had been comparatively content. Yes, he was loud and angry and frustrated and flustered, but things were generally going his way. His strategy up to that moment had been to conspicuously position himself as indispensable and, generally speaking, he had succeeded. But here was a battle best fought covertly. While he enjoyed a well-earned week off, I'd be invited to disgrace myself further by failing as the resident carer. He and Grainne would discuss the sorry situation over free drinks while he went after the deeds to the house.

I was astounded at how quickly I metamorphosed into my eleven-year-old self. Connor sneering at me with his vicious fight-starting face. Revulsion at the very sight of me. But instead of taking it all on like I used to when I was a boy I saw the man behind the mask instead. The clever frightened bully. The master manipulator capable of making the very puppets he controlled love him for it. And then I saw my own behavior in him and I didn't like that at all. No wonder I'd gone into advertising. It was the perfect occupation for someone trained in the art of covert manipulation. As the ridicule rained down I remembered my father's courage when he resisted my vicious alcoholic fits of rage. Even through the befogged windscreen of my careering juggernaut, I remembered being impressed to see that there was someone willing to stand up to my bullshit. Could I provide my brother with a similar epiphany?

It was official. He was gone for the week.

Brian dropped him at the bus station so he could go and annoy Grainne in Ballina. Meanwhile it quickly became obvious that the newly liberated territory would require careful governing and exhaustive administration, and though I was unsure about how to proceed, I was determined not to complain about it. Sacrifice and service. That was the AA code. Try to be of service. I had nothing better to do for my last week anyway and it was more practical and much cheaper than going on my own.

Mother was surprisingly mercenary about the whole thing. It didn't seem to matter who did what as long as she was taken care of. She began kissing me. Quick little pecks like an inexperienced girlfriend. She had never been so affectionate when she was alive. Brian became stoic and set his jaw against the inevitable battles ahead. I googled *Alanon Ireland* (for the relatives of alcoholics) and found a meeting for him on Tuesday nights at 8:30PM. Not that he'd attend. He'd continue to spend his evenings couch-bound and blue-hued in front of his card game. Why would anyone volunteer themselves bodily to the cold wet walls of that house? What did he lack in himself that he allowed it? And who was really in charge here? I began to feel tricked. Like someone was laughing at me. Maybe I'd been wrong-footed into doing exactly what Connor wanted.

Was he *that* good?

Either way I had a tough week ahead.

Mother demonstrated an almost clairvoyant knack for waiting until I was about to sit down before demanding that a door be closed or an orange be brought or fuel be fetched for the fire. I had to remind myself that it was she who put together the original program that controlled all our interpretations of events. She was almost literally the motherboard. No wonder she was so good at finding sensitive spots to prod.

"Will you be getting an apple tart?" she asked innocently as I psyched myself up for the weekly shopping trip.

"Maybe. Yeah I'll look for one. We'll see."

"Because I'm not making one," she said before the chance to hurt evaporated.

Even in her half-alive state she could still instinctively orchestrate a one-two punch like this. She hadn't forgotten my near-obsessive fondness for her apple tarts and, having reawakened my hopes the day before that she might actually bake one for me like she used to in the old days, she was now effectively denying any such conversation ever took place. It was a test perhaps to see if the subject had any emotional currency still attached. I hid my disappointment without really knowing why. I couldn't allow her to know it was a sore subject because it might encourage her to bring it up again. This was how I remembered my adolescence. Never give her anything to work with. Keep it all in.

The doorbell shook me.

I had always been stupefied by her slick transformation when visitors dropped by and now, a quarter of a century later as I noticed a small white-haired woman through the hall door, Medusa drew a hairnet over her snakes.

"Answer that will ya pet?"

My nervousness concerning the imminent weekly shopping excursion was alleviated by the news that I was to be accompanied by my mother's one remaining friend, Shiela. I was a source of great surprise to Shiela, since she'd been told I was fat and bald.

Even so I was invited into her little green car.

"I'm taking you downtown," she said, mimicking a thirties detective. Or at least I think she was mimicking.

Compared to mother she was spritely, probably in her seventies. If I was going to succeed as the new carer, I needed her know-how. And she certainly knew how. Which biscuits were preferred, what brand of tea to come home with, the approved sweets, the correct lettuce, the accepted shade of brown for the bread. Connor had managed to make the weekly shopping excursion sound so intricate and stressful it was like diffusing a nuclear device. For once he hadn't exaggerated.

And I wasn't aware that mother's first appearance each morning was heralded by the ceremonial dropping of boots, handbag and walking-stick from the upstairs landing. The heart-stopping *phump* as they hit the hall floor exploded in my mind in the form of a self-centered thought: She had fallen and died and I'd be blamed for her death.

Did she do it on purpose? While I was fetching tea and biscuits for them both, ("Fill it up halfway with hot water and leave the teabag in it you clown.") I heard her tell Shiela that she was *breaking me in*. And as she descended the creaking stairs I learned how I had managed to fuck up her precious electric blanket settings and as a result she hadn't even had ".. . . . one . . . fecking . . . wink . . . all . . . night."

She witheld the punch-line for the foot of the stairs.

"Oh I wish Connor was here."

"Good morning," I said, determined not to rise to the bait.

But I wished he was here too.

Could I really take a week of this? After all, in New York I lived alone. Nobody bothered me. I'd broken up with countless women in favor of privacy and now here I was tethered to a relentlessly needy old hag who not only smelled of piss at the best of times but took an almost sexual pleasure in pointing out my defects. We might have been married. Something occurred to me. Had Connor tampered with the settings on her electric blanket? Why leave your constituency in good shape for the new regional president? Obviously I would now need to call him after only his second day away and beg him to come back. How gentle his journey home, confident in the knowledge that I had fucked up where he was already proven. He'd be magnanimous and forgiving. Let bygones be bygones. No need to rub salt into wounds. My last week would be a week of humiliation and ridicule by omission. There was no fucking way I was letting that happen.

But it was like being shoved onto a live cookery show without a script.

Suddenly I was baking lamb chops for three and fretting about whether to baste, marinade, season or grill. I googled recipies feverishly. Were my lamp-chops boring? Careful. Don't get too tricksy, she'd spit it out if it got too trendy. Incinerate and serve. That was the way ahead. I needed a meeting.

A Latvian who insisted on saying *Jaysus* every few seconds gave me a lift home. It probably made him feel more Irish than he had a right to. I had already walked halfway before he caught up with me in his car. How could he afford a car when he had just shared in the meeting that he was on disability? It turned out he'd been hit by a truck when he was drunk and had broken his back, after which he spent three years in a wheelchair and two more in physical therapy and now he was three weeks sober.

"Jaysus," I said.

He looked over at me approvingly.

Ashamed of my high-class problems I was grateful to him for a lot more than just the ride home. We shook hands meaningfully. In Ireland, a recovering alcoholic is like an undercover agent in enemy territory.

"One day at a time," I said, slamming the door heroically.

I immediately tripped over something and fell. Since my last visit home rubbish bags had become the subject of careful curation. New European regulations required them to be reverently positioned for weekly collection. Heavy fines encouraged compliance. And since bonfires could now be spotted *from the sky* households risked retribution meted out with almost divine accuracy. Mother related these concerns with the awed conviction of a medieval villager. The result was that sacrifices were dutifully placed beneath twinkling sky and under the feet of mortals such as myself. The neighbors probably thought I was back on the booze.

Neighbor 1: "He was always fond of a drop."

Neighbor 2: "The same fella would drink off a sore leg."

The next day I heard my name called from the living room and when I walked in my mother was sitting on the ground like a fifties starlet smiling sweetly up at me. She'd fallen over again. I waited for the gush of guilt and remorse that would surely follow but none came. She might have been a piece of furniture that I lifted and replaced. If I ever wrenched an accomplishment from the jaws of adversity like a job or a raise or an award, her response had always been the same.

"Oh that's great, but don't tell Connor or he'll be jealous."

When I was growing up Connor was my idol. Maybe this explained the depth of my rage towards him. There was a sense of betrayal involved. Like I'd been lied to. He was the reason I went into advertising. I'd make it big and then we'd fucking see. But all the awards and the six-figure salaries were useless if I couldn't brag about them. So yes, fuck him and his kitty.

We began to correspond. She had married impetuously because she felt lucky to be asked. I allowed this to mean she'd never been fucked properly. I certainly hoped so.

My phone vibrated.

It was a message from jacquleine124.

"The irony is not lost on me that my limp was caused by a lack of oxygen at birth."

This referred to the title of my first book, *Diary of an Oxygen Thief,* and its source was a pretty girl from datemedotcom who was already insisting on picking me up from the airport. Why was the idea of a girl with a limp such a turn-on? Perhaps because it meant the normal rituals could be dispensed with. If she was damaged, I could be my unadorned self. Her facebook page provided me with more pictures and yes she had a lovely body. All creamy-skinned, long-haired and ladylike.

But with a limp.

We began to correspond. She had married impetuously because she felt lucky to be asked. I allowed this to mean she'd never been fucked properly. I certainly hoped so. While I let her wait the prerequisite hour for a reply I emailed a fantasy scenario to the tutor of French film: We are browsing in an East Village bookshop .... Between the shelves you hold my gaze and provocatively lick your fingers but instead of turning the page your hand descends under your skirt .... The book tips forward ...."

If she replied even halfheartedly to such overt filth, sex would be agreed to before we even met.

"Monsieur, I love the idea of holding your ... erm ... gaze in a bookshop."

But even so Jackie jostled the Francophile sideways with her limp.

Her approach was darker somehow and she required less lying to.

I walked over to the farm where I'd spent my summers as a laborer and even got misty-eyed at some of the memories I found there. Mons Hanarahan, so-called because he was a mountain of a man, able to achieve in a day what a crane would take a week to do. He drowned himself in the River Nore after his beloved greyhounds cannabalised each other while he walked them. He jumped between the frenzied dogs and ended up with a perforated eyelid. Even with his eyes closed one pupil was visible. But the barn we built was still standing. A Taj Mahal to wheat and potatoes.

The rest of the day passed unnoticed until late afternoon, when I couldn't get the oven to work. Flashback to an ad agency in London. The crucial presentation is in two hours, the printer is jammed and the client is en route. I dusted off my mantra: *Panic Beautifully*. But back then it had only been my salary at risk. Now it was my entire way of life. If I couldn't at least match Connor's coping skills I was nothing more than a bad ad for AA. And having already invested twenty years of my life in its manifesto, failure was not an option. Mercifully, Brian called to say he'd been delayed at work, and this being one of the few acceptable reasons in mother's mind for a delayed dinner, I used the precious time to refry the pork with a plate covering the pan, effectively creating an improvised oven. It was the equivalent of using the color copier instead of the printer.

But would it be *done* enough for her scorched palette?

Later as she shuffled back to the living room leaning more heavily than usual on her walking stick she managed to blame my cooking for her latest ailment.

"That shite went straight to me knee."

My first task on awakening each morning was to remove any evidence of being there. Having stowed away my camper-bed, duvet, pillows and sheets in the *good room*, I cleaned and reset the fireplace; actual ignition required authorization.

Rummaging through the firebox for newspapers to bundle up and burn I found a familiar-looking handwritten letter that began, "Dear Ma ..."

I felt the thrill of reading someone's private thoughts. Maybe it was from Connor. If so, I'd be exonerated for reading it since I needed to understand him better if I was going to help with his addiction. But as I looked for a postcode or an address I realized why it looked so familiar. I'd written it. A couple of years earlier while still in the process of breaking up with Marian, I put my thoughts down on paper. Nothing unusual about this ,since I kept a journal, but this was the only time I put those selfsame unedited thoughts in an envelope and mailed them to my mother. I blushed as I read a particularly sensitive passage. Embarrassment gave way to rage. Most mothers would treasure such a record of their son's tribulations and preserve them in the unknowable compartment of a handbag. But not this one. Here it was with the rest of the discarded reading material waiting to be burned. More worrying was the fact that ordinarily Connor lit the fire. He'd probably already memorized the juicier bits. I might well have supplied him with enough material for an uproarious comedy routine.

It would have been the last straw if I hadn't already given up on the place.

Instead it confirmed my decision to treat my remaining time there as service. An activity-holiday. Like working on a farm or volunteering a week of your time to help the less fortunate. I checked and rechecked the train times to Dublin like a miser counting cash. I was prepared to stay up all night rather than oversleep and miss the earliest train. I couldn't believe it had all gotten as overt as it did. In the past I'd always managed to hide my disgust for the duration of my visit. In fact that was exactly what I'd done for the first week but I just couldn't withstand the accumulation. My pipes burst. Disgust was too weak a word for it. Pure undistilled vitriol surged inside me looking for an outlet and Connor instinctively knew how to provide it. As my older cooler brother he had as much influence in my creation as my parents, if not more.

He had been the one I emulated.

I taught myself to play drums because of him. I went to art school to impress him. I yearned to *be* him. I saw how effortlessly popular he was and, yes, if I'm honest, how good-looking. Better looking than me. Better looking than any of us. And most of all I saw how mother worshipped him. All he had to do was appear in a doorway and the sound of her happy laughter filled the room. It was as if they were having an affair while the rest of us pretended not to notice.

And it didn't help that I was told on more than one occasion that I was unintentional.

A mistake.

There was a suspicious gap of seven years between Grainne and I while they were all born within a year of each other. Should I even be here? And yet here I was all these years later still competing for a turn at the wizened maternal nipple. Instinctively, I shoved the letter into my pocket when I heard the sickening *phump* in the hallway and my name pronounced with obvious annoyance by the enfeebled little shithead already halfway down the stairs.

"Why're you so grim?"

There had been an actual smile on her face when I first appeared because a quick survey of her realm from the upstairs window confirmed that the precious rubbish sacks were correctly placed outside the castle walls. She was probably about to praise me for having done something right but I couldn't take the credit since it was almost certainly Brian's doing. I could have used the good PR but I couldn't risk the scandal. I looked at her standing there half-dead. Was I just a thin-skinned alcoholic seeking new reasons to feel sorry for myself or was this in fact a gnomish little cunt?

Six more dinners to cook and five more fires to light before being released back into the world. What was I thinking? Why was I even doing this? I began to blame my AA sponsor for the needlessly long duration of my visit. I would never have stayed so long had it not been for his suggestion.

"It'll be good for your mom to see her son . . . and not just for a few days."

But that was before I knew Connor would be home. I had no doubt that it would have been a more kindly remembered visit if I had left after the first week. Maybe it was a good thing that it all came out into the open. And *mom* could have cared less who was there as long as she was taken care of. As long as she wasn't put in a home. I needed another meeting.

Meanwhile mother soiled herself again.

Thankfully I was in the middle of my meeting when it happened. Brian tried to help but had apparently made the situation worse by complaining about the stink. So much so that mother was in tears when I got back. I tried to console her but even as she leaned against me for what might have been the beginnings of a hug I detected the bittersweet scent of piss and shit slicing at my nostrils.

I couldn't see Connor mopping up shit.

A life lived in Ireland consists of being passed from the publican to the priest and the priest to the publican until such time as they both handed you off to the undertaker. Sheila revealed, as she drove me in her green car to the chemist to pick up mother's weekly supply of pills, that her late husband had been a Funeral Director. It was understood that his funeral would be an advertisement for her taking over the business. The idea had a certain gothic elegance to it and while I fretted about how best to work this into my woe-torn Irish play it took a few moments for me to realise that my eighty-six-year old mother's best friend was an undertaker.

Did she make similar visits to numerous other octogenarians? On one level it was selflessness cheerfully volunteered, but on another it was classic salesmanship. A decent funeral would cost at least eight thousand Euros. Not to be sniffed at in any economy. Did it matter? If you were going to be buried and someone had to be paid to do it then why not let your best friend have the gig? But how long had Shiela been my mother's best friend?

Only recently as far as I could tell. Did she have any younger friends? She dropped me off at our house and I watched her drive away, a vulture in a headscarf.

And I couldn't help noticing two large bottles of Valium on mother's list of otherwise unpronounceable drugs for which Connor would no doubt find a use when the hangovers got to be too much. I handed over the bag and she took an uncharacteristic moment out of her busy schedule as cunt-in-residence to thank me for everything I'd done since I'd been home.

"Thanks pet you've been a brick."

Either I had shown it was possible for someone to achieve the impossible standards Connor had set or, like a war criminal sensing armistice, she was making terms.

Meanwhile the girl with the limp continued to enthuse.

Having read my books she knew how much importance I attached to a shapely ass and she fretted now that I wouldn't like hers. I already knew it would pass muster since I'd looked up her Facebook page and found a photo of her wearing shorts. I bowed my head the better to inspect it. Tabernacle and supplicant.

And through no fault of her own Madmoiselle Julie began to behave like my girlfriend. I confessed that I had a desire to have children that spoke French. The language, already beautiful, became even more musical to me emitting from the tiniest of throats. But when she replied that she *absolutely loved this idea,* I immediately felt married. This was when I agreed to allow Jackie, her ass and her limp to meet me at the airport the next day.

It was a good time to talk to mother about how best to handle Connor. I helped her feel better about the fact that the house wasn't worth quite so much in the present economy and that this meant he had less incentive to carve it up into a bed-and-breakfast.

"Why? D'ya think he'd . . . ?"

"All I'm saying is, you should make sure you know where your check book is, OK?"

"That's what Brian said . . . ahh no he's not like that. He's jealous of you, you know?"

She *was* playing me.

But I was able to look more kindly on her now that I felt grateful to be leaving.

It was becoming obvious that caring for someone else's mother was a simpler proposition than caring for your own. Maybe Connor would get sober. That would solve everything And then it occurred to me almost as quickly that this was the last thing I wanted to happen. If he got sober I'd no longer have the moral high ground. I'd just be the mistake who visited every few years and he would once again be the golden boy. As it was he effectively shamed himself every time he drank and I was the last person to want that to stop.

I had actually begun to enjoy lighting the fire and preparing the food and even cleaning the house. These chores acted like stabilizers in my day, correcting the wobble. Did we have enough tomatoes? What about the fire? Was there enough coal in? Eggs? More Ambrosia rice? She likes her Ambrosia rice. Tea bags? What was I missing? Lettuce. Was there lettuce? Did she have enough sweets? How were we for potatoes? Had I butter enough for the following day? Sheila was due for another grocery trip . . . but hang on . . . an understocked kitchen would make Connor's return all the more awkward. Mother now talked about getting rid of him. She even sanctioned my brilliant idea of anonymously calling the social services to condemn him as an alcoholic. This would immediately render him ineligible. A devastating coup de grâce dealt from the comfort of a Bus Eireann window seat and all in the name of protecting my defenceless mother from her manipulative son.

But which one?

I had spent one week in Connor's shoes and only just managed it. Why shouldn't he come home and take care of his mother? And why shouldn't he get some money for it? Who was I to decide how someone lived? Or died, for that matter. Better an imperfect son than a hospice full of strangers. My motives were much more murky than I wanted to admit. I have the kind of mind that would kill me if it didn't need me for transportation.

In this case to New York.

on the b-38

Steve Dalachinsky

what are you waiting for / get covered / start here /
a gift of happiness or risky listening?
ya never can tell / drivin 26 yrs / 47 / nice humble guy
surprised / caught a heart attack / here today gone tomorrow
let them do the work / short trips / i had the last one
old man got shot just like that / lost his life / just like that
bird cage / i can't use that bird cage / like the door closed
i feel so claustrophobic / 14 yr olds with 350 magnums

& they call the b-7
7th heaven
it's a good run.

Ecce Homo

Evelyn Bencicova

Behaviour of a vulnerable human body. The expression of human kind in a simplified situation, raised to the surface. Archetypical behavioral patterns of a human in a society, yet not adjusted to the repetition of the previous experience.

—Evelyn Bencicova

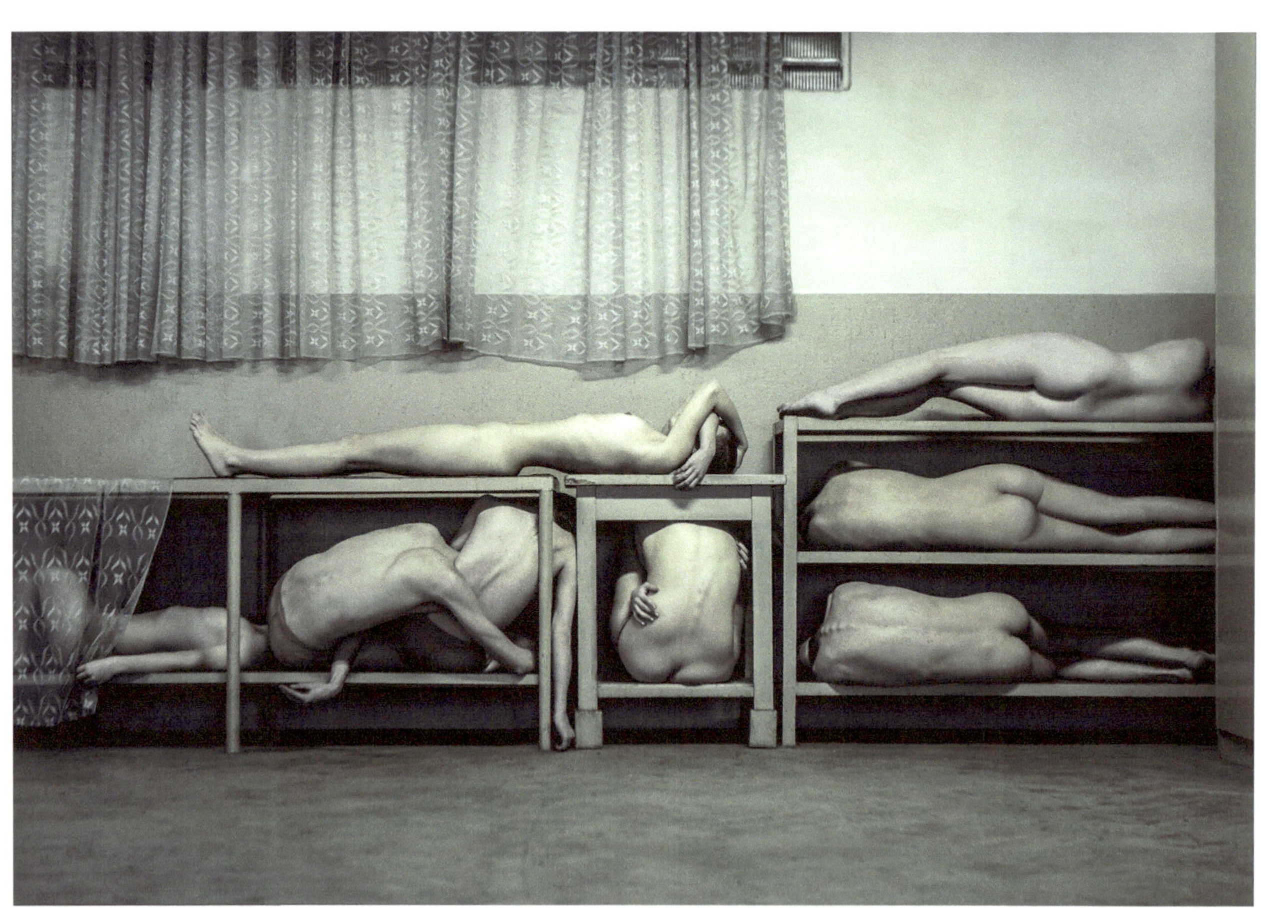

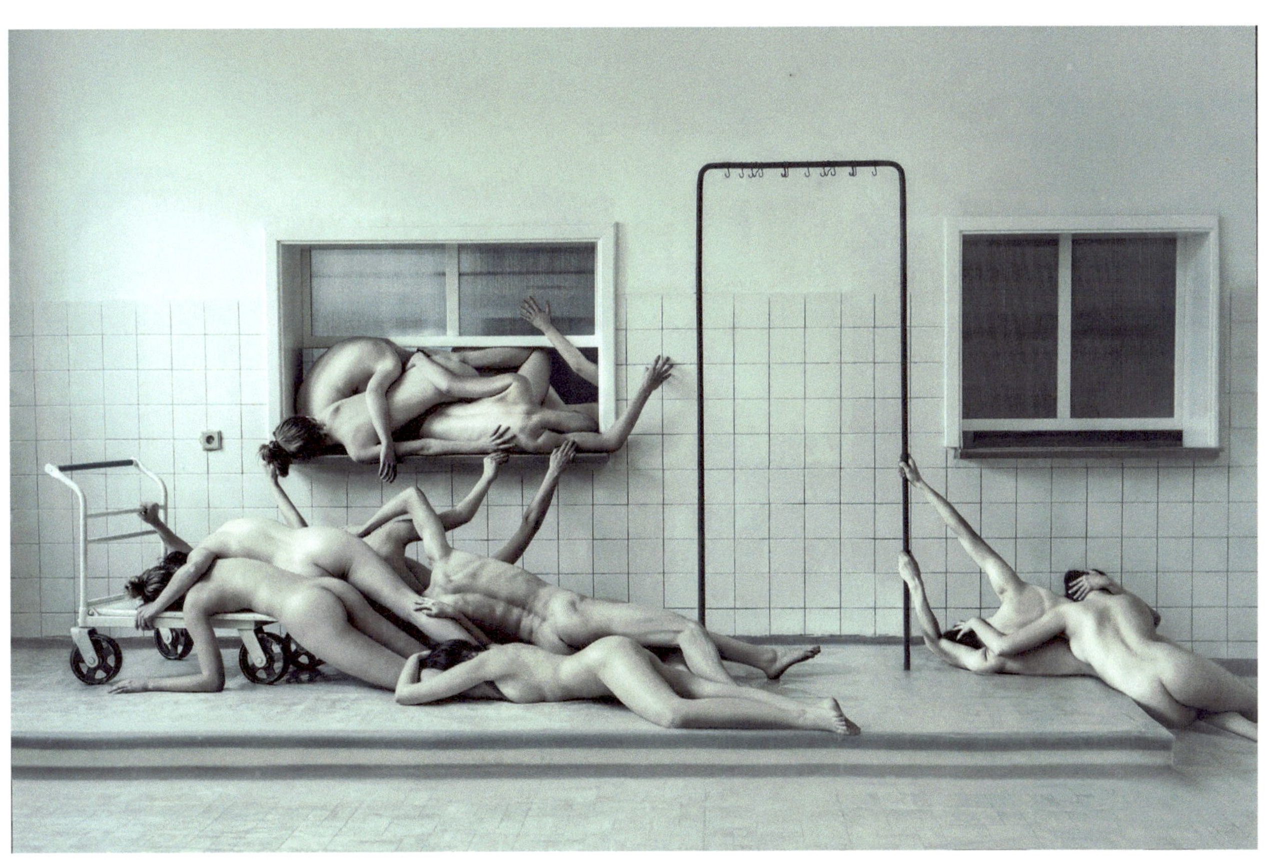

The "I Love Everbody" Tour Diaries

Maggie Estep

October 5th, 1994

We're leaving on tour in a few hours. Me and Pat and Julia will ride in Julia's big black truck and Steve and Keith, the Road Manager, will ride in the "Boy Car," a little white rental car. It's not deliberate gender division, just worked out that way.

Steve likes to drive at the speed limit and make very few stops. Us girls like to go 90 miles an hour, pee every 40 minutes and go to malls we find along the way. Neither Pat, Julia or I grew up around malls, so we're making up for that now.

Later, October 5th, Boston

We're sitting at the club in Boston eating Middle Eastern food. It's not that good, but it's free. We just soundchecked, and the sound was horrible and muddy, so we got depressed about our appaling working conditions and Julia said: "Why play? Let's just kill ourselves now."

October 6th, Northampton

We didn't kill ourselves. We played. It was kind of weird. We have the goofiest audience in the world. They're anywhere from 12 to 50 years old, and the only common thread is that they're total freaks, and they think I'm the Queen of the Freaks.

This 40ish fat woman gave me a bunch of pairs of panties. She was with her son, who was about 15 with a lot of pimples and a Bon Jovi shirt. He gave me a fruitcake. I don't know how that's supposed to make me feel.

This really cute, tall boy came up to me and said: "May I kiss your boots?" I laughed and said: "Oh, sure." Then, incredibly enough, he got down on his knees and really did kiss my boots. Then he stood up and walked away. I was, like, "Wait, where you going? Come back," but he just wanted my boots, not me.

October 7th, Montreal

So we eventually got to Canada and the Canadians are sexy, so it was worth it all. We got to the club and a dozen cute Canadians were waiting to help us lug our gear inside. Usually club people just stand around watching you hump gear, but these Canadians are great. We love them.

My fan Dominick the Accountant came to the show. Came backstage after we played. He had a briefcase, and in it he had all these accountant papers that he wanted me to autograph, but then he saw Pat and decided he was in love with her instead, and he stalked her all night. Meanwhile, Pat had seen this 50-year-old woman with grey hair hanging out in the bookstore next door, and she'd gotten a big crush on the woman because she was reading a book on Spirituality. Pat has this big thing for 50-year-old women who have grey hair and read books on Spirituality. I guess it's an acquired taste. Anyway, Pat wasn't into the accountant, and he finally left, depressed and in love with a spiritual lesbian guitar player.

October 10th, Rochester w/ Hole

It was our first gig opening for Hole, and now I never want to play for 100 deadbeats again.

We walked onstage, and 2000 writhing teenagers started screaming and trying to touch us. The front row was all girls, and they all had that tight-t- shirt-and-barrettes-in-the-hair look. I don't really understand the barrette thing. Little pink plastic barrettes were a bad idea when I was 7, and they're a much worse idea now. But it's OK; the barrette girls loved us, and their boyfriends kept pawing me and Julia's legs. They started moshing when we played "Fuck Me. "This was the first time anyone had moshed to us. So that was good.

After playing, we lounged in the dressing room waiting for Hole to go on. Little Frances Bean

Cobain was poking around back there, and it was eerie because she actually looks like Kurt Cobain. She was wearing big huge earmuffs so the loud music wouldn't scorch her little ears. Eventually, Courtney came in and she and Frances Bean and Eric, the guitarist, and Drew Barrymore, his girlfriend, all started throwing hunks of cantalope out at the audience.

Courtney is the indisputable Goddess of Rock. She was wearing a pale blue, see-through mini night gown, 9-inch, black patent-leather spike heels and frilly white underwear that peered out from under her pale blue nightgown. Her mouth was painted a big crimson slash, and she strode onstage, sneered, propped her long leg on the monitor, and started howling into the microphone. Little Frances Bean Cobain stood on the side of the stage, waving and saying: "Mommy! Mommy!"

?, Buffalo

There we were onstage, doing "Hey Baby," and I just went blank, completely forgot what the words were and just stood there on the stage looking confused. So the set was kind of downhill from there. The Barrette Squad still moshed, but I felt like a retard anyway.

After the show, we sat around in the dressing room saying, "Maybe we should just kill ourselves now." I know suicide's not supposed to be funny, but for some reason it is. So is bulemia; we've got this running gag about changing the name of our band from I Love Everybody to That Bulemic Moment. Or we could call the band Maggie Estep and Am I Fat?.

So we joked about suicide and bulemia, and then we got on the road and drove all night. The malls were all closed and America was asleep. We listened to Johnny Cash and ate half a dozen tootsie pops.

October 28th, On a Plane to Memphis

I'm flying to meet the band in Memphis because I just detoured for 2 days to play a 17-year-old poet in this low budget movie in Delaware. I'd never acted in my life, and I'm 31, so I guess it was a stretch. But they put barrettes in my hair, made me wear some ill-fitting pants, a tight t-shirt and some pink lipstick and presto, I was 17. My first line was: "Haven't you heard of me? I'm really famous."

And I pulled that off just fine. So now I"m flying to Memphis.

I'm stuck in the middle seat between an army guy and a guy who does some kind of urinary tract business. The guy is reading a report on the subject of Sphincter Urological Prosthesis, I'm not kidding. I don't know what a prosthesis in the sphincter would feel like, but I wouldn't think it would be nice, and can you possibly imagine devoting your life to that kind of thing?

October 29th, Memphis

Courtney was indisposed last night and cancelled the show, but we played anyway, and so did the other opening band, Veruca Salt. The singer girl from Veruca Salt is a big snotball. The rest of Veruca Salt are nice though. So we went first, then them. The Barrette Squad ended up giving me all the flowers and stuffed animals they had brought for Courtney so I made out just fine.

Before the show, me and Pat and Julia went into a weird Pizza place on Beale Street which is this famous blues Street. I hate the blues, but of course Pat and Julia love the blues, so we walked down Beale Street. We went into this little pizza joint. They were playing James Brown, and the place was empty but for a few old skinny black men sitting in a corner squinting and smoking. The lady at the counter was really mean to me because I ordered a sandwich, as opposed to pizza, and that meant she actually had to make something. She slathered it in mayonnaise even though I asked for no mayonnaise. So then I stood by a table wiping off mayonnaise, and all the skinny old black men stared at me. James brown was singing "Sex Machine."

Some kids found me after the show and made me autograph dollar bills and flyers and stuff. One boy had me sign his forehead.

October 29th, New Orleans

We had a really long drive down to New Orleans, and we hate all the CDs we have, so we ended up listening to a voodoo seminar on talk radio. We found a mall, but we didn't have much time so it was the quickest mall expedition in history. Me and Julia raced into Victoria's Secret and fanatically tried on lingerie, bought none, then raced back out to meet Pat in the parking lot. Pat had bought a book on spirituality.

Now we're in this weird hotel in the suburbs of New Orleans. We almost didn't find it because it looks like a hospital. Then it turned out it actually *is* a hospital. It's a hotel adjoining a hospital. They think of everything down here.

We passed through the bayou country on the way here, and it was beautiful: washed-out wood houses propped on top of the water, and shrimping boats everywhere. Old people sitting around with crinkled faces, just sitting there, watching the sun go down on the bayou.

October 30th, New Orleans

Last night's show was pretty weird. The audience stared at us. I know they're *supposed* to stare at us, but it wasn't a good stare.

Afterwards, we were hanging in the dressing room, and our friend Kate from New York showed up. She had Michael the Rock Critic with her and also this guy Tony, who's a journalist from Atlanta, and looks like he should have been in *Interview with the Vampire*.

Me and Julia and Pat and Steve were depressed and only half-heartedly joking about suicide and bulemia, but Kate and company cheered us considerably. Tony the Vampire amused me by playing with Hole's deli platter, and making sandwiches out of white bread, potato chips and mint jelly.

Courtney came into the dressing room after our set, and she gave me a dirty look. Some girl was there who follows Hole around everywhere. She was wearing this interesting see-through maroon dress and Courtney said, "I like that dress."

So the girl took it off, and Courtney took her own dress off, and they traded dresses. There were about 20 people in there, but both girls stripped down to their garter belts and black lace bras anyway. Courtney's body is like a superhero's: enormous tits, no hips or ass and legs that go on for miles. Everyone stopped what they were doing and watched Courtney in her underwear.

October 31st, Highway in Texas

We just stopped at a horrible diner, where me and Pat ordered shrimp gumbo which was really disgusting and looked like raw sewage. Julia ordered catfish and it came smeared in paprika. The only thing that was really good was the peas. The waitress hated us because we kept ordering side orders of peas.

Truck drivers in Mac trucks were fucking with us all night. They kept trying to push Julia off the road. "Julia, I think they want you off the road because you're driving slower than them, and they want to rush home and put on big bunny suits and have sex with their wives."

"No," Julia said, "They want to pull off at the next rest stop and put on big bunny suits and sodomize each other."

"That's not funny," Pat said. Maybe there's a bunny suit in her past. I don't know.

We pulled into a Holiday Inn and slept for a while before getting back on the road, then me and Julia had a big fight, and she called me a "little bitch tyrant" because I got mad that she and Pat were late getting up.

November 2nd, Austin

I checked my messages, and I'd gotten a message from my little sister, saying she got her tongue pierced. She could barely talk because her tongue was swollen. I called her back and asked her if it was a sexual thing. "What do you mean?" she said

"Well, don't people get their tongue pierced as a sexual thing?"

"No, I just did it 'cause it looks good," she said.

"Oh," I said.

"Well, I gotta go Maggie," she said then, clearly thinking I was a total moron for not knowing why she got her tongue pierced.

We had an OK show last night. They didn't start moshing till the very end of the set though. Then a bunch of 12 year olds were looking for us trying to make us autograph their foreheads, and I escaped into the dressing room and ended up sitting on the couch talking to Patti, the drummer from Hole. She had this great fuzzy backpack and we ended up comparing the contents of our backpacks. Mine was all practical stuff: a hairbrush, paper, a pen, lipstick and tootsie pops. In hers, she had a huge plastic rat autographed by Anne Rice, a miniature plastic rat with a bow around its neck, three pairs of boxer shorts and a picture of Jodie Foster. "That's what I would like for dessert," Pattie said, pointing to the picture of Jodie Foster. "Oh," I said.

"What would you like for dessert?" Patti asked.

"Cake," I said. I guess I'm boring.

So Hole went on stage and Courtney spent 2/3rds of the show talking to the audience. "I've had it with you little fucks, everytime I try to stage dive, somebody sticks their finger up my ass. Then they go, oooh, I had my finger up Courtney's ass and it stinks."

Julia and Jim, the drummer from Veruca Salt, were off in a corner flirting. Julia's been turned on by him since she found out he went to Yale. It's not so much that he went to Yale, but rather the combination of being a drummer and having gone to Yale. Keith, our road manager, thinks there should be a Playgirl spread of Ivy League drummers. Our own drummer Steve is an Ivy League drummer, and Keith is a drummer in a band and he's an Ivy Leaguer too. Personally, I don't go for Ivy League Drummers. I guess it's an acquired taste.

So, Hole went on stage and Courtney spent 2/3rds of the show talking to the audience: "I've had it with you little fucks! Everytime I try to stage dive, somebody sticks their finger up my ass. Then they go, 'Oooh, I had my finger up Courtney's ass and it stinks.'"

I'm not sure the Barrette Squad really ever stick their fingers up her ass, but I guess it's something to talk about.

November 2nd, Dallas

We all sat around in the dressing room, playing our favorite new game, which is to come up with new band names.

We're getting tired of "Maggie Estep and Am I Fat?" So Pat has a new one: "Maggie Estep and Gay Sex." Pat saw the headline "Gay Sex" on the cover of *The National Enquirer,* "Nicole Simpson's Last Days: Gay Sex, Drugs and an Affair with OJ's Best Friend." Pat, who of course *is* gay, thinks that "Gay Sex" is just the funniest phrase in the world. Now when we're hanging out backstage, we talk about Gay Sex. It's a sure way to get the mean Veruca Salt girl out of the dressing room.

November 3rd, Plane from Dallas

Last night was the best gig so far. I think we actually did better than Hole. The audience threw condoms and cigarettes at us, and I threw water on them, and we all bonded so much it was like a having a huge orgy with 2000 teenagers. So that was good.

Now we're done with the Hole tour. This woman sitting next to me on the airplane just asked me if I was in Dallas on business—which freaks me out because that means, I look like I do business.

"Yes," I said, "I was in Dallas on Business. I'm in a

Rock band called Maggie Estep and Gay Sex. We're really good." That wiped the smile right off her face. She pinched her lips and turned back to reading *Vogue Magazine* where there was a big spread of fashion models with little plastic barrettes in their hair.

Excerpt From Lollapalooza Tour Diaries

August 24th, 1994, Phoenix, AZ

It's 120 degrees here, and the sky is huge. In spite of the heat, they seem to be big on poetry in Phoenix. I read four poems then almost passed out from the heat. My t-shirt was soaked with sweat and some weird fan boy started following me around, trying to buy my t-shirt. Finally, I was saved by Torment the Drag Queen, who is now the official poetry tent MC. Torment came and stood between me and my loopy fan boy and told the fan: "Get down on your knees and lick my shoes, then we'll see about Maggie's t-shirt. "

The guy scratched his head for a second then turned and walked away. I kissed Torment's powdered cheek and lay down on the dirty grass and tried to recover from borderline heat exhaustion.

August 25th, San Diego

I performed a bunch of times, but nothing all that exciting happened.

I was lying on a couch in the Breeders' dressing room when Evan (the guy whose job it is to make juice for The Beastie Boys) saw me and said I looked sick, so he brought me into the Beasties' dressing room and made me a huge carrot juice.

The Beastie Boy I Have a Crush On was hanging out and we talked for a while. He told me he thought he'd seen me in an airport three days earlier. I said it wasn't me, but I was secretely pleased that he was hallucinating visions of me in strange airports.

Liz the Poet and I ate together. The catering tent was set up inside an indoor parking structure and all the food smelled like gasoline.

Liz was wearing a t-shirt with a picture of a kitten on it. Above the kitten Liz had written "LIZ: Poet, Cunt, Whore." Liz is not one to mince words. She has a poem called "All Women are Whores." And one called "My Country, My Cunt," which she and Torment, the Drag Queen, do as a duet. Liz says "My Country" and Torment says "My Cunt."

Liz is having an affair with a guy named Joe. Joe's official job title is "Snowman Roadie." He's in charge of the 8-foot paper-mache Snowman that L7 have on stage with them. He and Liz are crazy in love.

Now it's about 9PM and I'm riding with The Breeders on their tour bus and we're heading for L.A. Me and Levi, the Breeders Road Manager, are having a love affair, but we're trying to keep it a secret so I'm not going to write about it.

August 27th, San Francisco

Performed four times today, and it went pretty well. I taped a copy of me and my band's CD to my ass every time I went onstage. Then I'd turn my back to the audience, point at my ass and say: "This is my promotional device, and this is my CD. Please buy it."

I went to do a set on the Second Stage. Sterolab were going on right after me, and right in the middle of my piece, their guitar player started checking his guitar tone really loudly, so I couldn't hear myself. I turned around and gestured for him to please hold it for a minute, but he just made a snotty face and hit a power chord. I finished my piece, threw the microphone at him, and stormed away. I hate Stereolab.

I stormed into the catering tent to tank up on coffee and bumped into Billy Corgan, the Smashing Pumpkins Guy. He was in an expansive mood. He gave me this big hug, sat me down and asked what the matter was.

I told him all my problems, and he gave me career advice, then said he'd come play guitar for me during one of my sets. Then, my fellow poets Wammo and Shappy appeared, sat down with me and quizzed me in depth about Kim and Kelly Deal, who they worship. So I told them about how Kim doesn't ever change her pants but is really a sweetheart. That was the clincher for Shappy. He doesn't change his pants either. Now he's got this big fantasy about him and Kim breeding and frolicking and never changing their pants.

September 2nd, Los Angeles, Day Off

Last night me and Levi and the Breeders caught a plane from Seattle to LA. The tour bus dropped us at the airport in Seattle, and Kim Deal didn't want to get off the bus. She was holed up in the back lounge, burning candles and figuring out Hank Williams songs on guitar. All the rest of us piled off the bus. Finally, Levi had to practically pull Kim off the bus.

The whole sorry bunch of us traipsed through the airport.

Everybody stared at us. By this point, Kim hadn't changed her pants in probably two months. And I don't really think she'd bathed, either. I don't know why. She still seems to sing and play guitar just fine though.

We got to The Roosevelt Hotel around 2AM. Me and Levi have this big suite with a view of Hollywood Boulevard and a throbbing neon sign that says "Roosevelt."

September 4th, LA

I hate LA. I can't go anywhere because I don't know how to drive and Levi is busy doing important road manager business.

Last night I got really stir crazy so I went down to the pool and furiously swam laps. Back and forth and back and forth, and then all of a sudden, I see this hand in the water. I totally freak out, swallow huge gulps of water, then come up gasping for air. Then I see that it's only Wammo the Poet, sticking his hand in the water, trying to get my attention.

"Wammo, what the fuck are you doing here?"

"I've come to rescue you. Liz told me you were stranded here so here I am."

So I went up to the room and put clothes on then went off with Wammo and Shappy and a few guys from the Lollapalooza coffee booth. They were driving around in this huge Ryder truck where the coffee people store all their coffee-making supplies in, and also live in.

We tooled down Hollywood Boulevard in the coffee truck. We went over to Liz's house and from there walked to Liz's friend Joan's house. Liz's friend Joan really liked me even though I was in a surly mood.

She gave me three cups of coffee and some bananas ,and quizzed me about my brief acquaintance with Courtney Love, who she worked with a few years back.

Wammo got drunk. Liz and Joe the Snowman Roadie were kissing in a corner. The coffee boys got drunk. Me and Joan talked. The sun started to come up, the sky turned pale blue over the palm trees. I felt better. Joan's friend gave me a ride back to the Roosevelt. Levi was sound alseep.

September 5th, LA, the Last Show

I have a horrible cold and performed only once. Billy from the Pumpkins played guitar for me. He was wearing a big straw hat that obscured his face and I introduced him merely as "My love slave Bob" but the audience wasn't completely fooled, and spent the whole time trying to figure out if that was indeed Billy Corgan, and they didn't pay attention to the fine subtleties of my new poem called "Your Poetry Sucks."

I watched The Beastie Boys for the last time and for the last time watched the way The Beastie Boy I Have a Crush On's pants sagged loosely over his very small butt. And maybe this is what I got out of Lollapalooza, a bunch of crazy new poet friends, and a possible sequel to the Stupid Jerk I'm Obsessed With: "The Beastie Boy I Have A Crush On Who Wears Ill-Fitting Pants That Sag Loosely Over His Small Perfect Ass And Basically Doesn't Give Me The Time Of Day But I Don't Really Give A Shit Because Frankly I've Evolved Beyond My Obsessive Phase And Besides, I Got Bigger Fish To Fry."

Yeah, that's it. That's what I got from Lollapalooza. What more could a girl want?

Contributors

Alan Kaufman is the author of two memoirs, *Drunken Angel* and *Jew Boy,* and a novel, *Matches.* He is the editor of *The Outlaw Bible of American Poetry, The Outlaw Bible of American Literature* and *The Outlaw Bible of American Essays.* His latest volume, *The Outlaw Bible of American Art,* will be released in Spring 2015.

Stephen Lack has been painting and exhibiting internationally for over forty years. A seminal artist from the East Village Scene of the 1980s, he creates work that runs the gamut from political and interpersonal dramas to seemingly benign landscapes of America's greatest era. The subject of an *Arts and Minds* profile for Bravo TV, he recently held a retrospective of his car-related paintings, "Autonation," at the Illinois State School of the Arts in Normal, Illinois. Stephen has also participated in the making of several feature films, most notably *The Rubber Gun*, with Allan Moyle; *Scanners*, with David Cronenberg; and *All the Vermeers*, with Jon Jost. His paintings are in many American and international collections.

Joshua Mohr is the author of four novels, including *Damascus,* which *The New York Times* called "beat-poet cool." He's also written *Some Things That Meant the World to Me,* one of *O Magazine's* Top 10 reads of 2009 and a *San Francisco Chronicle* best seller, as well as *Termite Parade,* an Editors' Choice on *The New York Times Best Seller List.* He lives in San Francisco and teaches in the MFA program at USF. His latest novel is *Fight Song.*

Celia Farber lives in New York City and is the editor of *The Truth Barrier,* a tiny literary website. In a past life as a magazine writer, she wrote for *Harper's, Esquire, Rolling Stone, SPIN, Salon* and more. She is the 2008 recipient of The Semmelweis Society's Clean Hands Award for Investigative Journalism. She has ghost-written several books and authored one: *Serious Adverse Events: An Uncensored History of AIDS.*

Anonymous has created award-winning work for respected advertising agencies such as Saatchi and Saatchi (London) and Fallon (New York). His first book, *Diary of an Oxygen Thief,* was described as a "dark-horse Williamsburg bestseller" by *New York Magazine* and is now in its third printing. The sequel, *Chameleon on a Kaleidoscope,* explores the world of online dating. Anonymous lives in New York City and is working on the third installment of the *Oxygen Thief Diaries.*

Sparrow lives in a doublewide trailer in Phoenicia, NY with his loyal wife Violet Snow. He is teaching himself to play atonal harmonica.

Lynn McGee's poems have appeared in *The American Poetry Review, Southern Poetry Review, Hawai'i Review, 2 Bridges Review, The Same, First Literary Review East, Literary Mama, Bluestem, Big City Lit, The New Guard, Ontario Review, Painted Bride Quarterly* and *Sun Magazine* among other journals. Her chapbook *Bonanza* won the Slapering Hol Press manuscript contest and her manuscript *Wheel of Ice* was a nominee for the McGovern Prize. She is a member of the online poetry group Brevitas and lives in Brooklyn, New York.

Steve Dalachinsky's work has appeared in journals on and off-line, including *Big Bridge, Milk, Unlikely Stories, Xpressed, Ratapallax, Evergreen Review, Long Shot, Alpha Beat Soup, Xtant, Blue Beat Jacket, N.Y. Arts Magazine, 88* and *Lost and Found Times*. He is included in such anthologies as *Beat Indeed; The Haiku Moment; Up Is Up But So Is Down: New York's Downtown Literary Scene, 1974-1992* and *The Outlaw Bible of American Poetry*. Dalachinsky is the author of many books. Among his recent ones are *A Superintendent's Eyes* and *Fool's Gold*. Steve writes a monthly column about music, "Outtakes," for *The Brooklyn Rail*.

Arthur Nersesian is the former Managing Editor of the literary culture journal, *The Portable Lower East Side*. Four of his plays have been produced off-off Broadway. *The Fuck-Up*, his first novel, sold over one hundred and twenty thousand copies. An adaptation of his second book, *Dogrun*, was just filmed and will be released next year (starring Heather Graham). His tenth novel, *Gladyss of the Hunt*, was published in May. He lives in the East Village.

Edward S. Robinson is the author of *Shift Linguals: Cut-Up Narratives from William S. Burroughs to the Present*. He has written a number of articles on the works of Carl Weissner, Kathy Acker, Geoffrey Farmer and Stewart Home. His work is also featured in *Azimute: Critical Essays on Deleuze and Guattari*, and he has contributed articles to *The Reality Studio*, *The European Beat Studies Network* and *Paraphilia Magazine*.

Dennis Gordon is a photographer and model creator whose primary subject is abandoned structures, particularly post-operative industrial buildings. Born in 1957 in New York, Gordon completed high school and embarked on a 36-year career with the FDNY in 1978. Through the '80s and '90s, Gordon resided in the Lower East Side, while undertaking stints as a performance artist and actor, while deepening his exploration of abandoned industrial sites across the U.S. His unique background as a highly decorated firefighter, visual artist and Buddhist elicited an invitation in 2014 to lecture at the Rubin Museum of Art. His current modeling project is a 1/87th scale reconstruction of post-apocalyptic America inspired by his early years in firefighting with the FDNY and life in the Lower East Side. He was featured in the Steve Buscemi documentary, *A Good Job: Stories of the FDNY*.

Marian St. Laurent, founder of Heavy Symbols, LLC, is a media consultant and cultural analyst.

Margarita Shalina was born in Leningrad and raised on New York's Lower East Side. Her essays have appeared in *Yeti Magazine, Brooklyn Rail, We'll Never Have Paris, Pulse/Berlin, ThreePercent.com, ZEEK* and the anthology *Forgotten Borough: Writers Come to Terms with Queens*. She provided the literal translation for Annie Baker's critically acclaimed adaptation of Anton Chekhov's *Uncle Vanya* (Soho Rep.). She is the translator of *The Duel* by Anton Chekhov and was a contributing translator for*Food Chain* by Slava Mogutin, *Pussy Riot!: A Punk Prayer for Freedom*, the anthology *St. Petersburg Noir* and the journal *Animal Shelter*.

About him, Allen Ginsberg said this: "Marc Olmsted inherited Burroughs' scientific nerve & Kerouac's movie-minded line nailed down with gold eyebeam in San Francisco." **Marc Olmsted's** work has appeared in *City Lights Journal, New Directions in Prose & Poetry, The Outlaw Bible of American Poetry, Signs of Life, Processed World, Bongo Chalice, Blue Satellite* and a variety of small press publications. His work includes two books, *Milky Desire* and *Résumé*.

Natalia Evelyn Bencicova is a 21-year-old visual artist exploring mixed media and photography. She grew up in Bratislava, Slovakia and currently lives in Berlin. She began taking digital photographs two years ago and is trying to discover the point at which the commercial and the artistic meet.

Deborah Pintonelli is author of a collection of poems, *Meat and Memory,* and a story collection, *Ego Monkey. Some Heart,* her debut novel, is represented by Mitchell Waters at Curtis Brown, Ltd. She has won awards from the Illinois Arts Council, PEN Midwest, and the National Association of Arts and Letters. Her stories and essays have been published by *Gargoyle Magazine, Web Conjunctions, Tribes, Unbearables Press, Criminal Class, Chicago Literati, Vida/Herkind,* the "First Time I Heard" series, and included in anthologies published by NYU Press, Autonomedia, Thin Ice Press, and Arbre a Cames Editions in France. She is currently working on a new novel, *To the Last Gay Man I Will Ever Love.* She lives in Chicago with her two children.

D. Scot Miller is a Bay Area writer, visual artist, teacher and curator. He is on the board of directors of *Nocturnes Review* and is a regular contributor to *The East Bay Express, San Francisco Bay Guardian, Popmatters* and *Mosaic Magazine.* He is currently working on a book of poems and a novel, *Knot Frum Hear.* He recently published an old-fashioned manifesto titled *AfroSurreal.*

Gretchen Faust is an artist and performer. She's had multiple solo exhibitions at the Pat Hearn Gallery in NYC and Greengrassi in London, where she is currently represented. She has performed at the Franklin Furnace and the Jack Tilton Gallery in NYC. She wrote regularly for *Art Forum* in the 1980s and 1990s, and now resides in Totnes, England.

Rebecca Weiner Tompkins has played and recorded acoustic and amplified four and five-string violin and viola with Karen and the Sorrows, Life in a Blender, Chief, Scott McClatchy, Patti Smith and many others. Her poems have appeared in various journals including *Poetry magazine, The Seneca Review, The Antioch Review, Ploughshares, Pequod,* and *The Mercury Reader.* In 2009 she gave a TED talk in Canterbury, Kent UK, "Sensing Convergences," which is also the title of a manuscript she's writing. After 25 years in the East Village, NYC she crossed the river to live near Prospect Park in Brooklyn, where she spends a lot of time wandering about with her dogs.

Maggie Estep was an American writer and poet who was best known for coming to prominence during the height of the spoken word and poetry slam performance rage of the early 1990s. She published seven books and released two spoken word albums: *No More Mr. Nice Girl* and *Love is a Dog From Hell.* Estep appeared on MTV's *Spoken Word Unplugged*, PBS's *The United States of Poetry* and HBO's *Def Poetry.* Her video for her spoken word track "Hey Baby" went into regular rotation on MTV and was highlighted on MTV's *Beavis & Butt-head.*

Estep went on to write many novels, including *Diary of an Emotional Idiot,* the Ruby Murphy mystery trilogy, *Gargantuan, Hex* and *Alice Fantastic. Hex* was named one of the *New York Times Notable Books* of 2003. At the time of her death, she had been at work for several years on *The Angelmakers,* a novel about 19th Century female gangsters and the founding of animal rights.

Maggie died from the complications of a heart attack on February 12, 2014. This issue is dedicated to her.

Sensitive Skin Books

on sale now at Amazon.com and select bookstores!

"[Watson] writes like someone who pushed himself to the wall, then pushed through it to the void and came back with stories to tell. Here he reclaims the Seventies, one of the more desolate of recent epochs, with the clarity of Proust, the balefulness of Bodenheim, and the raw honesty of an Iggy song."

—John Strausbaugh, author of *Black Like You* and *Sissy Nation*

"With prose unfurling like cigarette smoke bleeding into that cloud of half-forgotten memories forever shadowing missed opportunities that hangs over a noonday dive somewhere during the twilight of the last blown century, heartbreak rock-n-roll on the radio crackling in exquisite precision between am stations and windswept interstates, Carl Watson daydreams before silent black-and-white televisions in SRO lobbies or as he drinks himself sober in crumbling Chicago tenements. *Backwards the Drowned Go Dreaming* explodes the bleary-eyed myth of the American road."

—Donald Breckenridge, author of *This Young Girl Passing*

"Carl Watson's work is desolate poetry. He writes with sharp nostalgia for a past that really wasn't all that great. It feels like a stay in a down-and-out motel, but right on the other side of the paper-thin wall is transcendence. Watson never lets you forget that even in the most desperate situations, there is humor (even if it's mostly black) and greatness of the spirit."

—Emily XYZ, contributor, *United States of Poetry*

Black & White on Paper | 6"x 9" | 238 pgs. | ISBN/EAN13: 0983927146 / 978-0983927143 | List: $15.95

Barefoot in the Heart is a collection of transcribed oral stories of the Indian saint Neem Karoli Baba (Maharaji). It includes many anecdotes and first-person retellings of stories collected in India and in the USA over a period of 9 years by Keshav Das, including a small selection of unpublished stories originally intended for inclusion in *Miracle Of Love* by Ram Dass.

"Barefoot In The Heart is a divine raft to take us across the ocean of darkness to the glorious land of light. Every page is filled with Maharaji's nectar. Profound gratitude to Keshav Das and his collaborators."

—Jai Uttal

Black & White on Paper | 6"x 9" | 168 pgs. | ISBN-13/ISBN-10: 978-0983927129/ 098392712X | List: $15.95

"Inside this book you get *portraiture vérité* of bands in action. Banging away in rehearsal. The appreciative eye watching the battle of the bands as they try to navigate their way through the sometimes complicated maze of illusions, delusions and solutions of grandeur before asphyxiation and evaporation of all the notes into the air. I'm the wrong person to comment on rehearsal as I work in a more backward way. I don't care if a performance is anally-retentive-perfect because a computer can do that now. I'll work hard on something to a point then I stop, as what I want surprises myself, especially in a live situation. It's a viewpoint probably not shared by most of the bands in this book but that's what makes things interesting. It's up to others to state theirs and that takes us to the artist.

"David West hits the target dead center BOOM with his beautifully liquid renderings of NYC bands in rehearsal. Mr. West captures a scene in the late 1990s largely ignored. These aren't vacuous American Idols but musicians who are The Real Deal. Like a fly on the wall, David gives you an inside view from his own multifaceted eye. There is a dripping aquatic fluidity to his drawings. Mr. West is not afraid to let the ink, gouache, and watercolor run and flow, never betraying the nature of his medium. That's why he's The Real Deal. If you the viewer can't understand, appreciate and see that in his work then go out and get corrective eye surgery!"

—Monte Cazazza of Psychic TV

Full Color Bleed on White paper | 8" x 7" | 110 pgs. | ISBN/EAN13: 0983927170 / 978-0983927174 | List: $24.95

East of Bowery began as a collaborative web project between writer Drew Hubner (*American by Blood, We Pierce*) and photographer Ted Barron in 2008. It was subsequently performed as a multimedia performance with live musical accompaniment at The Gershwin Hotel and The Bowery Poetry Club. This is the first print publication of the project.

"Drew Hubner's prose and Ted Barron's photos are kin, at once raw and lyrical, grit and grace, which is what the city was like back then. The combination is magic, the essence of the time and place."

—Luc Sante, author of *Low Life* and *Kill All Your Darlings*

"*East of Bowery* is a sharply focused, street-level view of Downtown before the real estate agents started renaming everything."

—Steve Earle, author of *Doghouse Roses* and *I'll Never Get out of This World Alive*

"Drew Hubner writes like people used to."

—William Georgiades, *New York Magazine*

"The voice is loose, jazzy, and fast, the memories liquid and hot, avoiding the romance of macho drug memoirs with black humor, verisimilitude and a knack for the absurd."

—Kate Christensen, author of *In the Drink* and *The Astral*

Black & White on Paper | 6" x 9" | 154 pgs. | ISBN/EAN13: 0983927103 / 9780983927105 | List: $15.95

SENSITIVE SKIN #8

on sale at Amazon.com and select bookstores
PDF version available at sensitiveskinmagazine.com/downloads/sensitive-skin-8/

Featuring a rarely seen interview with **William S. Burroughs** by **Allen Ginsberg.**

With iconic punk photographs by **Ruby Ray**, art by **Tom McGlynn** and **Justine Frischmann**, music by **The New Monsters**, a comic written and drawn by **James Romberger**, writing by **Mike Hudson, James Greer, Thaddeus Rutkowski, Chavisa Woods, Jim Feast, Mark McCawley, Todd Colby**, and much more.

Full Color on White Paper | 8.5" x 11" | 118 pgs. | ISBN-13: 978-0983927150 | ISBN-10: 0983927154 | List: $24.95

SENSITIVE SKIN #9

on sale at Amazon.com and select bookstores
PDF version available at sensitiveskinmagazine.com/downloads/sensitive-skin-9/

SENSITIVE SKIN
The World's Greatest Journal of Art, Literature and Music!
Number 9 $19.95

John Lurie/Samuel Delany/Vladimir Mayakovsky/James Romberger
Fred Frith/Marty Thau/ Larissa Shmailo/Darius James/Doug Rice/
and much, much more . . .

Featuring an exclusive interview with, and music by, seminal guitarist **Fred Frith** (Henry Cow) the missing chapter from the latest novel by science fiction legend **Samuel R. Delaney** and a portfolio of paintings from actor (Stranger Than Paradise) and musician (Lounge Lizards) **John Lurie.**

Plus a memoir by **Marty Thau**, former manager of Suicide and The New York Dolls, new translation of poetry by **Vladimir Mayakovsky** from **Jenny Wade,** photographs of the seamy side of Tijuana by **Chris Bava.**and an interview with **Darius James** conducted by **Ghazi Barakat**, about his new documentary, *The United States of Hoodoo.*

The front cover is by reknowned illustrator **J.D. King,** and the back cover features a comic written and drawn by **James Romberger.** There's more writing, by **Doug Rice, Susan Scutti, Larissa Shmailo, Bradley Spinelli, Anna Mockler, Jesus Angel Garcia,** and **Aman Sabet,** as well as art by **Ha Young Kim, Marcin Owczarek, John Griffin, David West** and **Justine Frischmann,** and photographs by **Ted Barron, Ruby Ray, Hal Hirshorn, N.D. Koster** and **Geoffrey Ithen.**

Full Color on White Paper | 8.5" x 11" | 102 pgs. | ISBN-13: 978-0983927167 | ISBN-10: 0983927162 | List: $24.95

Charles Gatewood/Gary Indiana/Sharon Mesmer/Nick Zedd/ Peter Shear/Patrick O'Neil/Max Blagg/Tony DuShane
and much, much more . . .

SENSITIVE SKIN #10

on sale at Amazon.com and select bookstores
PDF version available at sensitiveskinmagazine.com/ downloads/sensitive-skin-10/

The issue features out-takes from the Wall Street collection by famed photographer **Charles Gatewood** (*Sidetripping, Forbidden Photographs*), fiction by downtown legends **Gary Indiana** (*Scar Tissue and Other Stories, White Trash, Horse Crazy, Gone Tomorrow*), **Max Blagg** (*Ticket Out*) and **Drew Hubner** (*East of Bowery*) plus work by Dead Kennedy's roadie and junky bank-robber **Patrick O'Neil** (*The Hold-Up*), radio host **Tony DuShane** (*Confessions of a Teenage Jesus Jerk*) newcomer **E.A. Fow** and South American novelist **Raul Serrano Sanchez** (*Catálogo de ilusiones*).

We're also proud to present poetry by Flarf pioneer **Sharon Mesmer** (*Annoying Diabetic Bitch, The Virgin Formica*), **Ron Kolm** (*Divine Comedy*), **Pete Simonelli** (*Night Sees You First, A Lonely War*) and **Michael Randall**, essays by **James Reich** (*Bombshell; I, Judas*), **Ronald B. Richardson** (*Narrative Madness*), cinema of transgression co-founder **Nick Zedd** and South African activist **Breyten Breytenback** (*The True Confessions of an Albino Terrorist*).

We also have a portfolio of paintings by rising art star **Peter Shear**, and music by **Steve Adams** (ROVA Saxophone Quartet), with additional art, illustrations and photographs by **Yves Marchand & Romain Meffre** (*The Ruins of Detroit*), **Ruby Ray** (*From the Edge of the World: California Punk, 1977-1981*), **Chris Bava, Megan Baker, David West** (*Music: Drawing Down the Muse*), **Jeff Spirer, Charlie Homo, Ted Barron, Justine Frischmann, Julie Torres** and **Tom McGlynn**.

Full Color on White Paper | 8.5" x 11" | 120 pgs. | ISBN-13: 978-0983927181 | ISBN-10: 0983927189 List: $24.95

© j.d. king

www.ingramcontent.com/pod-product-compliance
Lightning Source LLC
Chambersburg PA
CBHW040821050726
47507CB00021B/94

* 9 7 8 0 9 8 3 9 2 7 1 9 8 *